Date Due

Feb 25 '63			
Nov 21 '63			
Sep 27 65			
Feb 28 '66			
Jul 12 '66			
Oct 5 '66			
Oct 19 66			
Nov 3 66			
Nov 17 '67			
Apr 23 '68			
Nov 11 68			
OZ OCAON			
Dec 16 '82			
	PRINTED	IN U. S. A.	

Shakespeare the Dramatist

Elliott & Fry Ltd

UNA ELLIS-FERMOR

SHAKESPEARE
THE DRAMATIST

and other papers

BY

UNA ELLIS-FERMOR

EDITED BY

KENNETH MUIR

NEW YORK

BARNES & NOBLE INC.

First published 1961

822.33

XE

42 764
april, 1962

Contents

Preface

WHEN I WAS ASKED by Una Ellis-Fermor's executors and publishers to prepare for the press a volume of her critical essays, I gladly undertook the task because I had been an admirer of her criticism for nearly thirty years. This book contains a substantial part of the work on Shakespeare which promised to be her masterpiece.

My thanks are due to the executors, to Professor Kathleen Tillotson, to Professor Hardin Craig for his valuable advice, to Dr G. K. Hunter and Mr Ernest Schanzer for help of various kinds, and to Miss Judith Darbey.

Acknowledgements are due to the editors of the journals and to the publishers listed on pp. ix–xi for permission to include some sections of the book.

KENNETH MUIR

A select list of
the published writings
of Una Ellis-Fermor

I BOOKS AND PAMPHLETS

1 *Christopher Marlowe*, Methuen, 1927.

2 *The Jacobean Drama*, Methuen, 1936, Second edition 1947, Third edition 1953, Fourth edition 1958.

3 *Some Recent Research in Shakespeare's Imagery*, Shakespeare Association, Pamphlet 21, 1937.

4 *The Irish Dramatic Movement*, Methuen, 1939, Second edition 1954.

5 *Masters of Reality*, Methuen, 1942.

6 *The Frontiers of Drama*, Methuen, 1945, Second edition 1946, Third edition 1948.

7 *The Study of Shakespeare*. Inaugural Lecture at Bedford College, Methuen, 1948.

8 *Shakespeare the Dramatist*, Annual Shakespeare Lecture of the British Academy, 1948.

II EDITIONS

9 *Tamburlaine the Great, in Two Parts*. By Christopher Marlowe. *The Works and Life of Christopher Marlowe*. General Editor, R. H. Case, Methuen, 1930, Second edition 1951.

10 *Caelica*. By Fulke Greville, Gregynog Press, 1936.

11 *Essays and Studies of the English Association*, XXIX, 1944.

A Select List of the Published Writings

12 *The Arden Shakespeare*, Methuen, General Editor, 1946–1958.

13 General Editor's Preface in *Macbeth* ed. K. Muir, 1951, pp. vii–ix.

III CONTRIBUTIONS TO COLLECTIONS OF ESSAYS,
LEARNED JOURNALS, AND OTHER PERIODICALS

14 '*Timon of Athens:* An unfinished play', *The Review of English Studies*, XVIII, 1942, pp. 270–83.
'Literary History and Criticism: General Works.' *The Year's Work in English Studies:*

15   XXI, 1940 (1942) pp. 7–19.

16   XXIII, 1942 (1944) pp. 7–16.

17   XXIV, 1943 (1945) pp. 7–14.
'Critical Studies.' *Shakespeare Survey:*

18   1 (1948) pp. 118–22.

19   2 (1949) pp. 132–41.

20   3 (1950) pp. 130–7.

21 'Some Other London Productions.' Ibid., pp. 105–6.

22 'The Poet's Imagery.' Broadcast, reprinted in *The Listener*, 28 July 1949.

23 'Die Spätwerke Grosser Dramatiker', *Deutsche Vierteljahrsschrift*, XXIV, 1950, pp. 423–39.

24 'The Nature of Character in Drama', *English Studies Today*, 1951, pp. 11–21.

25 'Shakespeare and the Dramatic Mode', *Neophilologus*, XXXVII, 1952, pp. 104–12.

26 'English and American Shakespeare Studies', 1937–52, *Anglia*, LXXI, 1952, pp. 1–49.

27 'Some Functions of Verbal Music in Drama', *Shakespeare-Jahrbuch*, XL, 1954, pp. 37–48.

28 'Ibsen and Shakespeare as Dramatic Artists', *Saertrykk av Edda*, 1958, pp. 120–35.

A Select List of the Published Writings

29 'Marlowe and Greene: A Note on their Relations as Dramatic Artists', *Studies in Honour of T. W. Baldwin*, 1958, pp. 136–49.

30 'The Nature of Plot in Drama', *Essays and Studies of the English Association*, 1960.

IV TRANSLATIONS

31 *Three Plays.* By Henrik Ibsen, Penguin Books, 1950.

32 *The Master Builder and other Plays.* By Henrik Ibsen, Penguin Books, 1958.

Introduction

THE CONTENTS OF THIS BOOK have been selected from the above list and from unpublished writings, and I have attempted to bring together all the existing sections of Una Ellis-Fermor's projected book, *Shakespeare the Dramatist*. Only one section (VI. 2) has been omitted. A number of admirable articles have been excluded, some because they have been superseded and others because they are on topics which have been treated more effectively elsewhere. Several of the omitted articles are careful surveys of other people's criticism, one is an excellent review of Sir Laurence Olivier's performance as King Lear, another has survived only in translation. Two unpublished lectures have been excluded because the author herself seems to have been dissatisfied with them.

As several of the printed essays were extracted from chapters of the book, and as most of the passages omitted from them would have been restored by the author, it did not seem wise to segregate published from unpublished work.

This book therefore contains the British Academy Shakespeare Lecture, which is a revised version of the first chapter of the projected book and in some sense an outline of the whole, followed by six chapters of the book and the paper on 'Shakespeare and Ibsen' which might also have been included. The text of the printed articles has been followed where possible, except that nearly all the omitted passages have been restored, and that one or two readings have been accepted from the typewritten copies. The early essay on *Timon of Athens* (with some later annotations) and the paper on *The Two Noble Kinsmen*, although they would not have been included in *Shakespeare the Dramatist*, show the applica-

Introduction

tion of the ideas developed in that book to problems of authenticity.

Shakespeare the Dramatist was begun before 1948. A programme of work connected with it, written on the back of galley-proofs of *King Lear*, was originally dated 1952. The first extant scheme is dated October 1954 after several chapters had been written, and this scheme was amplified before October 1955. There would doubtless have been later modifications, but at this time the book was to be divided into six parts, and two of these parts were to be subdivided into chapters:

I. Introduction: What do we mean by 'Shakespeare the Dramatist'?
II. The Essential Dramatist.
III. The Mode of the Dramatist:
   1. Link between II and III
   2. The Two Modes of Communication
   3. Communication in Character
   4. Communication in Structure
   5. Communication in Thought
   6. Communication by Imagery
   7. Communication by Language and Verbal Music
   8. Conclusion.
IV. The Emergent Dramatist:
   1. Link between III and IV
   2. From Statement to 'Secret Impression' (Character, structure, Imagery, etc., Music)
   3. Underlying theme.
V. The Authority of the Dramatist.
VI. Appendix:
   1. On the use of certain words
   2. On inner and outer plot.

At the time of her death, Una Ellis-Fermor had completed Part II and drafted most of Part III and half of Part VI. We can tell, however, from the amplification of the 1954 scheme how it was proposed at this time to develop Parts IV and V. 'The Emergent Dramatist' was to deal with Shakespeare's 'evolution towards the essentially dramatic', and it was to show how, 'in each kind he practised, he led, not followed his contemporaries'. It was to show how Shakespeare proceeded from statement to secret impression, from an emphasis upon outward to the revelation of inner drama in action and ex-expression – in character, in plot, in imagery, and in verbal music. The last chapter in this part was to show that the underlying theme 'is embodied in the play, not "revealed", or, obviously, "expressed"'. The point to make in this chapter is that only when all has become a matter of 'secret impressions' can an underlying theme be fully contained or embodied in the play. It can then be portrayed or indicated at the secret level where alone it can exist in drama. Thus, whole and complete implication is necessary before a play can in fact have a 'meaning'. 'The Authority of the Dramatist' was to be an expansion of the last two pages of the British Academy Lecture.

The writing of the book was continually interrupted by her work as General Editor of the new Arden Shakespeare, and, in later years, by ill-health. But although we may deplore that the book was left unfinished, it is clear that all the points outlined above are contained or implied in the completed chapters. 'Completed' is a relative term, for Una Ellis-Fermor was a ruthless critic of her own work and she would doubtless have revised all the material included in this book, especially the unpublished chapters. Yet, even in its present form, it is a valuable contribution to our understanding of poetic drama in general, and of Shakespeare in particular.

Una Ellis-Fermor's work includes a pseudonymous volume of verse, editions of Marlowe's *Tamburlaine* and of Greville's *Caelica*, a pioneering book on Marlowe, two standard surveys of Jacobean and Irish drama, translations of some of Ibsen's plays, and a seminal volume of essays, *The Frontiers of Drama*. The best essays in the present book are worthy to stand beside the best in that collection, and her essay on imagery there fills a gap (III. 6) in *Shakespeare the Dramatist*. She was a subtle and penetrating critic of drama, especially of tragedy, and she was at her best in writing of Shakespeare because in herself she combined great intelligence with great integrity, and because she had a high conception of the function of art – 'changing the very being of man through education of his imagination', as she expressed it in her Inaugural Lecture:

> Art for life's sake, if you will, that life may become art; that we may become so endued with the poetic habit, that daily living becomes instinct with imagination, an act of worship, as is every act of creative art. This is the fruit of the true study of any major poet. Let us see to it that our study of Shakespeare keeps always this fact in mind before and above all others. For our knowledge of a great poet is, after all, not a purely personal concern. It is a little like Burke's vision of the social contract: 'Since it cannot be obtained between many generations, it becomes a partnership not only between those who are living, but between those who are living, those who are dead, and those who are yet to be born'. Scholarship may extend itself sometimes beyond the centre to the circumference; though always, if this is wisely done, it will bring back ancillary knowledge to enrich that central and essential understanding. But our part in this is, first and last, to maintain and to hand on that tradition of essential understanding as we ourselves received it. 'My sword I give to him that shall succeed me in my pilgrimage.'

Those words of Bunyan, quoted twice in her lecture, may serve also for her valediction.

I

Shakespeare the Dramatist [1]

IN SPEAKING TO-DAY OF Shakespeare the dramatist I propose, with your permission, to consider one question: To what degree and in virtue of what quality in his genius is Shakespeare a dramatist? What, in other words, constitutes the specifically dramatic quality in his writing and how nearly is that the native habit of his mind? For it is evident that, in the Elizabethan period, when conditions fostered the art of drama, many writers became practising dramatists who in another age would have sought another medium; Ben Jonson was almost certainly one of these and so in some degree was Marlowe on one hand and Webster on the other. Just so, during the nineteenth century, many poets as evidently diverted their imaginations from the drama, which offered them only an incomplete and inhibited form of artistic communication. Was dramatic expression, then, partly induced in Shakespeare, as it was in Marlowe, Jonson, and Webster, by the favourable conditions, the prevailing mood of the age? Or was it essential to his genius, innate in him, profiting no doubt by the coincidence of man and moment, but not prompted, as in some of his contemporaries, by the demands of that moment? May we, as a first step

[1] The Annual Shakespeare Lecture of the British Academy, 1948. A typewritten draft of this lecture, under the title 'The Essential Dramatist', has been compared with the printed version. One passage, added in manuscript, has been restored, in square brackets, in the footnote on p. 9. The draft opens with three paragraphs differentiating dramatic and epic poets from other poets and artists. These are partly based on Lascelles Abercrombie's *Towards a Theory of Art* and *The Principles of Literary Criticism*.

towards answering this (and so my initial question), look for a moment at the nature of drama, or, more precisely, at the nature of dramatic genius?

Clearly we are not concerned here with the obvious characteristics of the literary form that we call drama; these, though derivative from, are not the essential manifestation of, dramatic genius. If we remind ourselves of them briefly it is rather that, having so recalled them, we may set them aside before beginning to look for the generic and then the differentiating qualities of the art and of the artist. We are not likely to meet with disagreement, to need to justify ourselves, when we say that in a play which shows competent craftsmanship as a play, we expect to find at least three things: action, or a reasonably clear and coherent plot; characters, themselves the sources of this action, who convince us that they are human beings, such as we meet or might expect to meet; speech, the dialogue through which plot and character are revealed, which satisfies us that it is such speech as these men, meeting these events, might use. If one or other of these three is notably defective, we find a piece of work which fails as a play, whether or not it has in it fine poetry, subtle thought, or firm design. There is some noble poetry in W. B. Yeats's *Shadowy Waters*, but there is not enough action, in outward event or inner experience, to give it the vigour and immediacy of drama. There is subtle and sometimes searching thought in much modern drama, but such a play as Denis Johnston's *The Old Lady Says No* fails to move the audience – as a play – because the central figures are not imagined primarily as human beings. There is firm design and some understanding of character in Browning's *Strafford*, but the words do not strike upon our imaginations as they would if they were instinct with the life of speech at any level of experience. If, however, all these ends are duly served, the play will be at least a workmanlike piece of craftsmanship (it may, of course, be much more), even though the emphasis be laid on the action, as in *The Spanish Tragedy*, on the revelation of character, as in Maeterlinck's

Shakespeare the Dramatist

Aglavaine et Sélysette, or on verbal wit, as in Etherege's *Man Of Mode*.

To determine, then, what dramatic genius is in its essence, we must look below these formal characteristics, these outward signs of dramatic thought, and ask what are the innate powers of mind which lead a poet to apprehend life in terms of dramatic experience which, if they are not thwarted by circumstance or conditions, will certainly direct his artistic expression to dramatic, rather than to any other, literary form. We are not concerned, that is, with the nature of the average play (which, like the average novel, need not be a work of art at all) but, first, with the nature of dramatic art, and then with that of dramatic genius; the first of these may best be learned from the study of the major drama; the second can only be so learned.

And so, setting aside technical and formal considerations, we examine first the generic qualities which the great dramatist shares with certain other major artists and then those qualities or powers which differentiate the dramatist and drama. We call in evidence such dramas as, while fulfilling the technical demand, so inform it with the universal and the enduring that, when what is temporal and perishable has lost its meaning, an imperishable and eternal significance shines through, and Aeschylus speaks to men of to-day, not as an Athenian of two thousand years ago, but as a man whose essential experience is still ours. Passion, thought, and poetic imagination, unchanging even in the wreckage of the civilizations they worked upon, survive event and circumstance and reveal man's kinship with the indestructible spirit of which great art is an image. And it is somewhere here that we shall find our starting-point. Passion, thought, and poetic imagination are, I think, the generic characteristics of dramatic genius and we can trace their manifestation in the substance of drama, and, if we wish, in the form, through the work of all the greatest dramatists. How, then, do these manifest themselves in drama, and what is Shakespeare's portion here?

3

Shakespeare the Dramatist

It is perhaps upon the passion and intensity with which the dramatist apprehends the world of experience that great drama depends, in the first instance, for its power and its immediacy; though passion is, in the last analysis, inseparable from thought and poetic imagination, and these from each other. It is the intensity, first of his imaginative experience of the world about him, then of his artistic experience – the act of transmuting this into a work of art – that gives to the great dramatist his power to move men, to touch the depths of their imaginations, to free them, and to set at work the powers of life. Nor are there any narrow limits to the shape this mighty force may take when it informs the characters in a great drama. It may be released, or may appear to be released, almost without guidance, as in the terrifying whirlwinds of madness in a Lear or a Timon. It may be stifled, or appear to be stifled, in the marmoreal calm of the Chorus Leader in the *Oedipus at Colonus*: 'Not to be born at all Is best',[1] or in the deceptively prosaic utterance of Middleton's or Ford's tragedies, of Ibsen's late plays. A Macbeth, an Agamemnon, a Jocasta may, as men do in actual life, hold it with difficulty in some kind of restraint; a Clytemnestra, a Lady Macbeth, seemingly with less difficulty, may hide it altogether. A Medea, an Othello, a Borkman may, without crossing the border-line of madness, release a part of what is shattering the mind. It is the presence of the passion, not the mode or the extent of its expression, that matters, and it is our awareness of forces beyond our own imagination that strikes us into awe and receptivity in the presence of the *Agamemnon*, the *Oedipus*, *Othello*, *Lear*, or *Timon*. Whether it appears to be revealed or seems to be hidden is really of less moment than we think, for our subconscious minds, wiser in this than 'meddling intellect',

---

[1] *Oed. Col.*, 1225-8.

μὴ φῦναι τὸν ἅπαντα νικᾷ λόγον· τὸ δ'ἐπεὶ φανῇ
βῆναι κεῖθεν ὅθεν περ ἥκει
πολὺ δεύτερον, ὡς τάχιστα.

4

recognize and respond to the hidden as swiftly as to the manifest.

This power is not the prerogative of the dramatist; it will be found in varying kinds and degrees in all great artists. But though diffused or mitigated passion, though moments only of concentration are compatible with the highest reaches of art in other kinds, the dramatist depends upon it as the very matter of his. We recognize its working in the debates in the second book and in other isolated passages in *Paradise Lost*; but *Samson Agonistes* is instinct with it throughout. In Dante and in Goethe it is again intermittent, giving place to description, to meditation, to reasoned reflection, even to satire; in Wordsworth there is still less direct expression; it is diffused in the underlying groundwork of the thought; the solemn exultation of the music, in his major poems, its only outward sign. But in the great dramatists it is sustained and seemingly inexhaustible; Marlowe, Webster, Racine (in this among the greatest) suffer no dilution and little or no intermission. The power and comprehensiveness of their passion would alone distinguish the great masters of drama from all but the occasional companionship of their fellows. And here Shakespeare, as our instinctive choice of plays suggests, is with Aeschylus and Sophocles.

But the great forces set at work by passion are not undirected. 'God spoke to Job out of the whirlwind', and over the passion evoked by the intensity of his apprehension presides, in the major dramatist, the directing thought which gives us what has been called the logic of poetry.[1] The operation of thought, the effect of the continual discipline of contemplation or reflection, is harder to discern in drama than in many forms of art. And this we should expect, for it is inseparable from the differentiating quality of drama (of which we shall have to speak later),

[1] I am partly indebted for this phrase to Mr C. Day Lewis, who, in his recent work *The Poetic Image* (1947), discusses in Chapter V the function of poetic logic, referring back to the use, by W. P. Ker, of the term 'poetical logic'.

5

Shakespeare the Dramatist

that preoccupation with the life of man, doing and suffering, which affords – except in rare instances – but little opportunity for the direct expression of reflection. Such revelation as there is is therefore implicit and can often be consciously abstracted only by a deliberate consideration of the total effect of action, character, and sentiment interrelated within a given play held whole in the mind of the critic.

This is, in effect, to say that in some plays it cannot be abstracted at all, for nothing but the total play will give us its 'meaning'. What, after all, is the meaning of *Much Ado*? Or, for that matter, of *Antony and Cleopatra*? A governing idea, a sequence of thought, can, it is true, be traced in *Troilus and Cressida* or the group *Richard II*, *Henry IV*, *Henry V*, but even here thought and content are more nearly coterminous than it is always convenient to admit. The 'logic of poetry' remains, in fact, the logic of *poetry*, and thought is revealed, in each aspect of the play, precisely by the presence of the excellence proper to that aspect; if we consider the characters, we find in it the depth of Shakespeare's understanding of motive and human experience; if the structure, it is in the flawless relation of the form to its subject. If we look for a theme in Shakespeare's plays, we find none, other than the bottomless and endlessly extending wisdom that asks of his readers a lifetime's consecration to explore. The operation of thought, then, is easier to discern than the resultant thoughts; a man must be blind to whom Shakespeare's architecture spells nothing, but he would fall into as great a folly if he assumed that the operation of this governing and presiding intelligence must necessarily give indications which can be abstracted and restated as the conclusions of a philosopher, an historian, a moralist, or a psychologist. The dramatist's is an impersonal art; its ways are secret and his thoughts are often hidden in those ways. But the sign of thought, in profound and powerful, sometimes in prophetic, form, is in the strength and majesty of the work of art itself and each fresh exploration teaches us to recognize here the conscious and unconscious intellectual control of passion.

So it is (with reservations which will be noted later) with the thought of Aeschylus and with that of Sophocles, Euripides, Ibsen. It is true that in these a part (a progressively diminishing part) is explicitly stated in the commentary of the chorus or an equivalent modern agent; but the total thought remains coterminous with the content of the play, of which this is itself a part. And it is too easily forgotten that in the first and second and in some degree in the third of these dramatists there are formal and aesthetic relations between the choric odes and the rest of the play which reveal in terms of another mode some part of the theme and are indispensable to full conscious or unconscious apprehension of it.[1]

In all of these poets, then, the major dramatists of literature, the forces evoked by passion are directed by thought, serving to express it, as it in turn expresses them.

And so we 'enter that state of grace which is called poetry',[2] a mode of experience, a condition of mind which is inherent in and yet partially distinguishable from passion and from thought as they are from each other. By 'poetry' in this sense I would be understood to mean that apprehension of beauty which irradiates the mind of the poet, presenting order or form as an aspect of truth, and distinguishing it at that point from the mind of the philosopher or of the saint. This radiance, this sense of glory in things seen or felt or imagined and of the ultimate and underlying truth of which they in turn are images, is communicated to us in ways which again differ widely in each of the greatest dramatists. It is at work in the major lines of design which give form to structure and to character and in details of expression – imagery and verbal music. It is the

[1] On the relations between the choric ode of Aeschylus with the form on the one hand and the theme on the other, see H. D. F. Kitto, *Greek Tragedy* (1939).
[2] See again C. Day Lewis, *The Poetic Image* (p. 58).

Shakespeare the Dramatist

ever-present sense of significance in all things, of some hidden reality in them ever about to become manifest. Its clarity is at its height in the work of Aeschylus, of Sophocles, of Shakespeare, where design and detail are alike instinct with it; it is intermittent in certain dramatists second only to the greatest; though always there, it burns low and sometimes almost invisibly in Ibsen. Like passion, the poetic apprehension of the universe may reveal itself in drama clearly or more obscurely. From the time of his full maturity it never fails in Shakespeare's authentic work; in Ibsen, at the opposite extreme, it is sometimes so deep buried as to leave us blind to its working. Yet the imagery of *Antony and Cleopatra* springs, though with fuller potency, from the same faculty as the occasional overtones of beauty in *Rosmersholm*, and the secret kinship of the two is revealed by the solemn yet continuous presence of such overtones, side by side with clear and distinctive imagery, in such a play as the *Oedipus at Colonus*.

Such, then, are the generic forces that we discover if we look below the outward characteristics of drama presented to us by a normally constituted play and inquire what is the essential attribute of dramatic genius. But these, being generic qualities, are shared in varying degrees and relations by all great literature. What, then, differentiates drama from other forms of literature and the dramatist from other writers?

The nature of this differentiation has already been indicated in some of the suggestions we have made. Put briefly, it consists in this, that the dramatist (with whom up to this point we must be prepared to admit a certain kind of novelist) is concerned with the life of man acting and suffering. Here and here only can he rightly find his material. However far he may make universal his implicit theme, his subject remains man's experience, and all that he says or implies must be said in terms of this medium. From this there follow, almost as corollaries, two inferences. First, that the dramatist's mood, his attitude, will itself show a characteristic differentiation, which we may think of as

8

sympathy. He enters into the minds of his characters (ideally into the minds of all of them) and speaks, as it were, from within them, giving thus a kind of impartiality to his picture of life, sorrowing with him that sorrows, rejoicing with him that rejoices. In certain rare cases this may take the form of an equidistant detachment from, rather than active participation with, all his characters,[1] but this, for our purpose, is a distinction without essential difference. It is the equality of his relations with them all that is the essential feature. And in close conjunction with this inference we may draw a second. The dramatist's primary concern being man's life, acting and suffering, and his relation to this basic material being one of sympathy, the mode which offers him the fullest expression is direct revelation by the agents themselves. No other means will allow him so to concentrate upon the essentials of his subject, no other will present so economically the passions and thoughts of men as to leave men themselves, under due safeguards, to present them. And from what has been said of the nature of that sympathy which is a differentiating characteristic of dramatic genius, it follows that the genuine dramatist meets no obstruction in expressing his passion thus mediately instead of immediately,

[1] This is extremely rare in drama, even in comedy. (It is not to be confused with what is extremely common in most dramatists below the greatest, an imperfect distribution of sympathy, so that some of the characters, but not all, are treated objectively.) Middleton alone appears to preserve this attitude in tragedy and that only in the main plots of his two major tragedies. [Nor should we perhaps accept the appearance without inspection. For Middleton's pictures of the travelling mind lost upon a strange and sinister road of experience convey into the imagination of the reader the terror and the pity which do not come by chance but only from the operation of deep, if hidden, emotion. Middleton, like Swift, appears not to feel; but inasmuch as each stirs in reader or audience a powerful and painful response, the sympathy of the writer cannot be doubted.] Ibsen occasionally seems to achieve it, but this is generally found, on closer inspection, to be either a momentary failure of sympathy in one direction or the result of a deceptive concealment of an underlying but passionate sympathy.

9

as the passion of his characters, not as his own; nor in the fact that his reading of life can only be expressed indirectly and by implication (in such ways as we have already indicated), and that even his sense of the poetry that irradiates his universe is at the mercy of the people of his drama.

Now, just as the different dramatists, though fundamentally akin, differ somewhat in the balance and relation of these generic qualities we began by considering, so, it will be found, do they differ in respect of this differentiating characteristic of dramatic sympathy and the technical mode that follows from it. Dramatists differ in their power, or their desire, of maintaining equidistant relations with their characters; at one extreme we find Marlowe, who, in *Tamburlaine* and in *Faustus*, identifies himself with one or at most two characters and enters only intermittently into the others; at the other extreme we find Shakespeare, who speaks from within each of his creatures as it speaks. So also do they vary in the extent to which they express directly their own passion, their own perception of poetic truth, and make explicit or keep implicit their reading of life. Marlowe again is at one extreme in the first of these and Shakespeare at the other; in the second the extremes may be illustrated by Aeschylus on the one hand and Shakespeare again on the other. So far as his characters allow him, a dramatist may express with a measure of directness his emotion and his poetic delight. But those larger inferences from his experience which we call his reading of life can only, as we have said, be expressed implicitly, in terms of character and event and the relation between the two. In so far as he does in fact depart from this law, itself an inference from the differentiating characteristics of drama, in so far does he depart from the strict dramatic mode. This divergence, here possible to dramatists, may be briefly illustrated by the different methods of revealing thought through or independently of character and action. (Since, as has been indicated, the problems in the dramatic revelation of passion and of poetic experience are less crucial, the divergence in practice is less wide there and calls the less for illustration.)

Aeschylus, as is obvious, gives us in twofold form his comment on the world of his play; in one form it is implicit and dramatic, lying wholly within the dialogue; in the other, in the choric odes, it is explicit and to that extent non-dramatic, sometimes almost a direct statement of a theme. The two are complementary and in complete harmony, but each is dependent upon the other and neither alone would render fully his interpretation. This is true to a less degree of Sophocles. Euripides, perhaps simply because he came later in the tradition which had bequeathed the choric ode, but more probably because he instinctively laid more emphasis upon action and suffering, revealed his reading rather by the indirect, implicit method. More than any modern of comparable stature, Ibsen renders parts of his interpretation in terms of direct commentary, though he is dramatist enough to put suitable characters in charge of the operation.[1] Of the greatest dramatists of the world's literature, one alone, so far, has used the dramatic mode, and only the dramatic, for the revelation of his underlying thought. It is Shakespeare who baffles impertinent conjecture and unimaginative exegesis alike by affording us no re-expression of his implicit, dramatic utterance in terms of explicit commentary. The reading of life revealed by his plays cannot, as we have already noticed, be abstracted, for it is co-extensive with the plays themselves and can only be learnt by a lifetime spent in their world.

If, now, we look again at the properties of the resulting 'kind',

[1] Here the modern convention of dramatic plausibility may be partly responsible. Certain of the Elizabethans, who were not subject to the naturalistic convention, though poets of great dramatic force, availed themselves of the relative freedom of their dramatic form to use the equivalent of brief choric commentary without undue regard to the characters to whom it was assigned. Webster is adept at inducing his reader to accept this without realizing it.

those outward characteristics which, taken together, constitute the conventional forms of drama, can we discover anything more? I think we can, by this means, add something to what we have already said of the operation both of those generic forces and of those differentiating qualities which are at work in the mind of a dramatic genius. We may observe that they can transmute, not only traditional and conventional forms but even the limitations imposed not by convention but by the nature of the kind itself, and make both subservient to significant form.

When a traditional or conventional form comes into the hands of a dramatist of genius, when passion, thought, and poetic imagination have there expressed themselves in terms of sympathy and by means of direct presentation, we find the elements of a play (action, character, dialogue) transformed, so that each fulfils more than the bare functions necessary to make of the work drama rather than some other literary kind. Through the operation of those powers the relation between these elements becomes more fruitful; action or plot becomes significant form, itself an aspect of the play's meaning or thought; the revelation and grouping of character becomes the spatial aspect of the play's structure;[1] and dialogue or speech the vehicle for our necessary knowledge not merely of action and character, but of much upon which depends our understanding of the relations between the world of the play and the wider universe of which that world is a part. Contrast between scene and scene becomes in *Troilus and Cressida* an image of disjunction, in *Antony and Cleopatra* of synthesis; in the first play

[1] The spatial aspect of structure and the relation between spatial and temporal form in drama are discussed in detail in G. Wilson Knight's *The Wheel of Fire* (1930). 'A Shakespearean tragedy is set spatially as well as temporally in the mind. By this I mean that there are a set of correspondences which relate to each other independently of the time-sequence which is the story' (p. 3). (The theory is developed in the first chapter, 'On the Principles of Shakespearean Interpretation'.)

the theme is the discord of the universe, in the second it is the conflict in Antony's mind between an empire and a mistress, and the vastness of that empire images the magnitude of the conflict. The grouping of characters in each play serves the same end, somewhat as does the relation of colour and shape in pictorial composition; and imagery directly and verbal music indirectly relate the significance thus revealed within the play to that of the wider, surrounding universe.

When we consider such drama as this, which has passed beyond mere adequate craftsmanship to take its place among the great art-forms, we find that it, like all other arts, meets and conflicts with the limitations imposed by its form and seeks out means of transcending them. And it is the major dramatists, with whom we have been all along concerned, who discover and reveal to their fellows the possibilities inherent in the form, which can, paradoxically, enable them to transcend its limitations. Their discoveries may be defined by their followers or imitators, by those who are consciously or unconsciously taught by them, sometimes as branches of technique, sometimes almost as technical devices; but in the hands of the original masters they are the findings of far-reaching imaginative exploration. It is Aeschylus, so far as our knowledge allows us to judge, who perceives a further function of the choric ode, using it to refer outward, beyond the boundaries of the play's actual content, to a moral and spiritual universe of which his chosen portion of life is a significant part. But this is the least innately dramatic of all the modes of transcending limitation in scope, and what we have already said would lead us, even if we had not studied his work, to expect that Shakespeare would not use it. In fact, he does not. But since to remain in subjection to the limitations of a form is to write a work of art which may be the poorer for its submission, he finds his own ways to enlarge the content of his play, to deepen its significance, and to reach out beyond a given pattern of character and event to a universe of thought and experience of which they are but a representative fragment.

13

Certain of the means by which he does this we can in part discern, though our description of their working must necessarily be imperfect. The soliloquy (very differently used by most of his predecessors and contemporaries and by many of his successors down to the present day) allows him to let down a shaft of light into the hidden workings of the mind, to enable us to overhear its unspoken thought without in effect suspending the outward movement of the action or breaking the impression of the immediacy and reality of the dramatic world. The imagery in his dialogue, for which, again, the Elizabethan habit gave him precedent, allows him, without extending the body of the speech, to let those same words which convey to us our necessary knowledge of feeling, thought, or event convey simultaneously many other things which our subconscious minds apprehend even if our conscious thought does not, deepening and extending our perception, now of the mood of the play, now of the nature of a character, now of the significance of the action, now of the relation of the whole to that wider universe which surrounds it. The verbal music, all that we include in the effects of rhythm and pitch inherent in the words and disengaged from our language by Shakespeare's blank verse, have a similar function and work simultaneously with imagery to similar ends. He, moreover, can evoke, by rare and exquisite use of what may be called the overtones of speech and action,[1] something other than, yet simultaneous with, the words, images, and music which yet continue in their appointed functions. Each of these powers latent in the medium of dramatic dialogue was known to one or other of Shakespeare contemporaries; Shakespeare alone uses them all, and, at

[1] This use of what may be called the dramatic overtones, though it is as old as dramatic art itself, being akin on one side to irony and on another to the significant use of silence, is peculiarly skilful in some modern plays. The French *Théâtre de Silence* depends in part upon it for its effects; in Thornton Wilder's *Our Town* it is, if I am not mistaken, the principal vehicle of the theme.

the height of his power, simultaneously, and he alone to all the ends I have suggested. Of the great moderns, Ibsen is a master of the first and of the last; of the soliloquy which reveals the hidden thought of his characters and of the art which evokes from speech the overtones that reveal something related to, yet other than, that speech. But imagery tends with him, as never with Shakespeare, to pass over into the less dramatic mode of symbol, and verbal music is limited (though never destroyed) by his later dedication to the prose medium.

It is perhaps at this point that we realize how often and how nearly we have approached to begging the question in saying: 'This writer (or his method) is more nearly dramatic than that.' Can we now attempt some such statement without falling into that fallacy? Can we say that if, from our chain of hypothesis and deduction, we can abstract for ourselves an idea of what constitutes the innately dramatic mind, the mind that finds its expression in a mode which is fully and strictly dramatic, then such and such dramatists approach most nearly to this ideal? I think we can.

Clearly enough it has been to Shakespeare that we have been so often tempted to point. Even in a brief and cursory survey of the obscure movements of the great generic powers, we find, and I think we find justly, that Shakespeare, in the possession of the primal forces from which drama derives, is with the greatest. Yet already there, and still more when we pass to the differentiating characteristics of the art, he sometimes seemed to stand a little apart. We suspected, again somewhat in anticipation of the argument, that it is he alone who uses no modes but the dramatic; he alone who never steps out of his play to speak, disguised or undisguised, in his own person. Can we, with that in mind, point to any distinctive characteristic and say that this carries an artist to the heart of the dramatic experience and gives to his work full dramatic quality? Is there, in fact, in his approach to his material anything which sets apart the genuine dramatist, the man whose art is wholly dramatic from the first

15

moment of its conception to the last detail of communication? Is there a faculty which makes possible for him a special mode of artistic experience,[1] and that mode the dramatic?

If we look again at the distinction we drew between the dramatic and the other forms of great poetic art, we shall find at the same time both the explanation of our conviction that Shakespeare's art is the most consistently dramatic and the answer to this last question. The method of a given artist, while derived primarily from his instinctive choice of material, is immediately determined by his approach to it, and Shakespeare's method reveals the approach distinctive of the dramatic artist, a limitless sympathy with man acting and suffering. Because of this sympathy, the passion, thought, and poetic imagination which inspire all artists are, in the dramatist, determined towards the distinctive dramatic method, the direct revelation by those who themselves act and suffer. And when these primal forces of art are so determined they infuse the principle of life that transmutes convention and transcends limitation, preserving the art from sterility and renewing it phoenix-like from age to age.

When we apply our minds to the understanding of a character in a great play, attempting to enter into it with our imaginations as a great actor does in preparing to act it, what is it that we find? We find that the dramatist has so wholly imagined his character that what he has revealed within the framework of the play seems to be only a part of what he knows, just as what a man reveals of himself in any one series of his actions is but a part of what he is. We are accustomed to say that the dramatist has identified himself with Agamemnon, with Oedipus, with Agavé, with Macbeth, with Hjalmar Ekdal. We can, if we will, amuse ourselves by transporting the character to other periods

---

[1] I assume here the distinction between artistic and aesthetic experience drawn by Lascelles Abercrombie in *Towards a Theory of Art* (1926), and now generally accepted, the artistic experience being that involved in the act of artistic creation.

or situations, back into childhood or away into some other series of events and actions, and this frivolity is not without its use if it teaches us something of the fullness of that original imagining. We find, by degrees, that we can do this most often with the characters of Shakespeare's plays, for it is his practice to give us hints, not so much of events as of formative influences in the lives of an Edmund, an Iago, a Hamlet, even of so early a figure as Richard III. And so, returning to our study of the actual content of the play before us, we may trace the processes of the mind, as the actor must and does, through scenes in which the continuum of speech is interrupted and find again that the guidance given us is enough because Shakespeare's understanding of the mind was whole. We can, if we use our imaginations faithfully in the interpretation of the clues that are given us, follow the thought of Bolingbroke through the scene before Flint Castle and the deposition scene, in both of which, but for a brief speech or two, he is silent through long periods; just so we may divine the links between the broken phrases in Lady Macbeth's speech in the sleep-walking scene, and relate each utterance to some moment in the foregoing action, the memory of which now calls it forth. All this we can do with the central figures in Shakespeare's plays as with many other dramatists (for some who are not the greatest treat in this way their central figures).

But can we now, disengaging Shakespeare's work again from the matrix of great drama we have been studying, discover anything more? What if the actor or the reader change his part from Macbeth to Lady Macbeth, is not what we have said still true? Obviously it is. Then is it true also of Duncan, of Banquo, of Macduff – even of the unfortunate Malcolm, encumbered as he is by the third scene of the fourth act? We must, I think, agree that it is. And are there not two murderers, men who appear but for a brief moment or two to plan with Macbeth the assassination of Banquo? Are we not given just enough in-dication of the world they live in to arrive at a momentary

Shakespeare the Dramatist

understanding of the springs of their motives and to remain convinced that though only a slender arc of each personality enters the frame of the play, the circle is complete beyond it, living full and whole in the poet's imagination? And so we might pursue the investigation through all the authentic plays of Shakespeare's maturity. In all of them we find this imaginative sympathy, this identification of the poet himself with every character in his drama.

But this is not the end. We said a moment ago that the thought of Bolingbroke in certain scenes of *Richard II* [1] was potentially revealed to us even in those passages where he is silent and other men are speaking, and that we, while they speak, can continue to identify ourselves with him. And we can, if we wish, make each of these other men in turn the centre of our attention and then, when they in their turn are silent, their thought will similarly be revealed to us while others speak. It is not a matter merely of Shakespeare's identifying himself with each in turn, with each man as he comes to life in speech, but with each man's momentarily hidden life for so long as he is within the framework of the play and, if necessary, beyond it. The self-identification with each and every character is not only whole but simultaneous. This, I submit, is the genuine dramatic mode of thought, the fundamental quality which reveals the innate dramatic genius, and it is this, I believe, which distinguishes the essentially dramatic from all other kinds of genius. How rare this is, a moment's reflection will assure us.

If this is true, then we have in Shakespeare not only a dramatist but *the* dramatist, the only one in the great company of dramatic poets who is wholly and continuously dramatic. The only one, that is to say, in whom there are to be found, in the highest degree and uncontaminated with other modes of thought, both the generic powers and differentiating qualities of dramatic genius, and a resultant art whose mode and whose methods are wholly dramatic.

[1] *Richard II*, II. iii. and iv.i.

18

Shakespeare the Dramatist

The artistic experience of the essential dramatist thus differs from that of other artists at a point very near its roots, and the response of human beings of many races and of most recorded ages indicates the depth of the relation between common human experience and the best-loved of the arts. For the paradox inherent in the dramatist's attitude to man, his subject, is also the source of his power. In his vast, impersonal sympathy lies one solution of the problem so long familiar to mystics: 'Teach us to care and not to care.' And the dramatist having, like the great mystic, in some measure solved this problem, speaks as one having authority.

For the communication thus made is distinguished from that of the imperfectly dramatic by a factor whose significance it is almost impossible to over-estimate. 'This even-handed justice', this universal sympathy which has at once the balance of impersonal detachment and the radiance of affection, gives to the record made and to the reading of life implied a power of assurance beyond that of any utterance short of the affirmation of the mystic. Convinced at once of the depth and of the range of Shakespeare's experience through his imaginative understanding of the passions and thoughts of men, we are convinced no less of the truth of his perception through this single quality, the universal sympathy of the genuine dramatist. For it is this which, operating without bias, reveals in the mind of a man the shadow of the divine attribute of simultaneous immanence and transcendence. The confidence felt by generations of men of many races in the reading of life implicit in the total body of Shakespeare's plays depends in the last resort on the fact that not merely did he know what is in man, but that he knew it as a dramatist. 'If this is true', it was once said of a concerto of Bach, 'all is indeed well.' Because, in the man whose genius is wholly dramatic there is no prepossession, no prejudice, no theory, because no matter of common experience is left out of the account, his ultimate assumption, still implicit because still dramatic, will carry the same assurance as the revealed vision of

Shakespeare the Dramatist

the mystic, and will carry it in times and in the places the mystic does not touch. This is the supreme function of the dramatist. That Shakespeare has fulfilled that function beyond all others is only to say in another form that he, beyond all others, is wholly a dramatist.

Note

Two sections are missing between this chapter and the next. The first of these was to discuss 'the contrast between inward and outward'. The second was to be 'a general description, first by means of extremes, perhaps, such as Shakespeare and (*Cato, Mourning Bride*, Corneille, Ibsen? Checking Corneille by Greeks to be sure they are of the other kind)'. This note is accompanied in the draft scheme by a marginal warning: 'Don't let this become too doctrinaire. Don't labour it. Sound casual and discover it, rather [than] demonstrate it. And don't overdo anticipation of other chapters, esp. Conclusion.'

II

The Mode of the Dramatist

OUR CONCLUSIONS SUGGEST THAT the most direct way to an understanding of the nature of drama may be in the study of character and that it is the dramatist's approach to and universal sympathy with his characters that leads him to those methods of communication that distinguish his art from all others. It may be that after considering this we shall find confirmation from other aspects of a work of dramatic art (such as the plot, or arrangement of the incidents) and of the dramatists' technique as it is there revealed. For we remember, too, that Aristotle says plainly that the plot is the first essential.[1] But though Aristotle's claim may be true of the initial inspiration, of which some critics believe him to be speaking here,[2] the common reader's response to the resultant work of art appears to reverse this order and approach instinctively through character. Perhaps the present generation of readers is particularly ready to take this road; given our prepossessions, our immediate tradition in Shakespeare criticism and the habits this has bred, the most familiar way into the understanding of a play is by what we call character. This happens to be the gate near which the greater number of us dwell.

What then is 'character' in drama and what do we understand when we talk of its functions? What is the relation, for the ideal reader, between what he meets in life and what he

[1] *The Art of Poetry*, 6. 11.
[2] An interesting comment on the probable order of imitations in the process of communication will be found in Lascelles Abercrombie's *Principles of Literary Criticism* (1932), pp. 100–1.

21

meets in drama, life being, after all, the material from which the dramatist's image of an action derives and upon which it works?

Just[1] as a work of art differs as a whole from the raw material which is its source, so much its various parts or aspects differ from the corresponding aspects of that material. In that particular branch of the art of literature which we call drama, plot or action, for instance, is not identical with a series of actual events, though it has a special relationship to it; nor is dialogue identical with actual conversation, however cunningly it may contrive to appear so; nor 'character' with character. That aspect of a play which we may, if we wish, abstract from the whole and think of as a 'character' has travelled a long way from the original source of inspiration. It took its rise, in the dramatist's imagination, from his experience of and not-necessarily-conscious interpretation of human motive, emotion, thought, and action, as they appeared to him in life and at a particular moment. It was resolved, by the artistic process, into a conception or form held, unexpressed, in his mind. Next, or it may be half-simultaneously, this was transmuted into communicable form in terms of certain conventions, conventions mysteriously potent in their operation upon the imaginations of the recipients – in this case readers or audiences – communicating to them a proportion of the poet's original experience, the proportion varying, of course, in any given conjunction, in accordance with his power to communicate and theirs to receive.

From this it follows that we must not demand, when we approach dramatic character, too limited or too immediate correspondence with character as we meet it in life. We do the artist wrong when we apply the test of superficial resemblance and use that as our criterion of his fidelity to truth. The revelation of character, like any other branch of dramatic technique,

[1] The remainder of this chapter was printed as 'The Nature of Character in Drama with special reference to Tragedy' after being delivered as a lecture at a Conference at Oxford, 1951.

should not, properly, attempt to deceive us into believing that what we have before us is fact itself or a direct deduction from fact. Yet this must not be taken to imply that it is illusion, if by illusion we mean something incapable by its very nature of leading us to truth. Dramatic character, like dramatic plot, is an image on the grand scale, and it is the function of imagery to evoke in our minds certain perceptions, realizations, emotions, which are themselves aspects of an underlying reality, not to present us with a scientific statement of fact, an abstract from that perceived reality.

This is, of course, a commonplace of aesthetics, but its truth has sometimes eluded critics, largely perhaps because certain dramatists have themselves denied it in practice and in their theories, misleading dramatic criticism, not so much about their own experiment as about the real nature of this aspect of dramatic technique. For drama occupies a somewhat anomalous position among the arts in that it appears at first glance to be inherently representational, and the habit of certain of its weaker practitioners in the recent phase of its history has confirmed this impression in the minds alike of audiences, critics, and subsequent dramatists. Fidelity to surface appearance, in character as in other branches of dramatic technique, has been given, in popular and in critical opinion, an honourable estate as a mode of presentation to which the evidence does not, I think, entitle it. A host of honest, workmanlike dramatists of the second rank have practised it assiduously and with the best of artistic intentions; one at least of the first rank seemed for a time to set his seal upon it. But drama, which, because it is transmitted to us in the theatre through impersonations by living men and women, appears to come nearer to the actual than any of the other arts, is in fact debarred by certain fundamental laws of its nature from any sustained attempt to present surface appearance. Its brevity alone would make this impossible, even if the deeper-lying demands of passion and thought did not add their weight to the swift momentum. We are thus confronted with another of those paradoxes that beset dramatic aesthetics. The art which in its proper sphere of the theatre seems the most nearly immediate of all is forced, in obedience to that law of concentration without which it would not seem immediate, to present action, character, and even speech itself in terms which, upon investigation, turn out to be profoundly unrealistic.

The attempt to deny this fundamental necessity of drama, which is, properly, the basic dramatic convention, is of very recent growth. Without the weighty authority of Ibsen, it is doubtful whether the diligent output of the everyday dramatist of the mid-nineteenth century would seriously have disturbed our acceptance of the grand, ancient technical tradition of what Aristotle classed as tragedy. But in a few of his plays (and how hard it is to persuade our generation that they were only a few!) Ibsen did in fact appear to lend his genius to an experiment the results of which bewilder our judgements to the present day. Some half-dozen sinister accidents then combined to make the small group of plays from *Pillars of Society* to *Wild Duck* his most influential in those countries whose own influence was to count for most in twentieth-century dramatic criticism. Small wonder that the early work of Dumas *fils* seemed to be confirmed in its implications, or that the Galsworthies and the Brieux of the twentieth century followed. A revolution occurred and it seemed for a time that major drama could be written in terms of everyday life, whether of action, character, or speech. And this meant in the domain of character that the brevity of drama must now be circumvented in a new way, not as before by offering an image of the hidden reality at the roots of life, but by an abstraction from it, a statement of conclusions drawn from it by a deductive process and presented in terms of diagrammatic or self-explanatory character. The great artists do this with consummate cunning and Ibsen offers us a long line of characters in whom this procedure is justified because they have been forced by temperament or circumstances to think about themselves, sometimes to know themselves, but

The Mode of the Dramatist

always to become lucid and facile in explaining themselves. Brand, Karsten Bernick, Lona Hessel, Nora Helmer, Mrs Alving, Pastor Manders, Oswald Alving, Regina Engstrand, the brothers Stockmann, all have this capacity for self-examination and in each it seems at the worst plausible, at the best inevitable. But the great hinterland of the unknown self to which the Greeks and the Elizabethans had access, the domain of great poetry and of the poet or the mystic in the common man, was closed. The counter-revolution which Ibsen himself began in the late plays with the studies of Solness, Hilda Wangel, Rosmer, Rebecca West, and John Gabriel Borkman is not yet stabilized; we have lost our way, as W. B. Yeats long ago realized, to the sources of the living imagination in drama. We are confronted with what appear to be two valid and alternative ways of revealing character, the expository and the evocative, but in fact the first of these is not valid and cannot lead to full, profound, or poetic revelation. Like the lovers in Yeats's story we have attempted to put our knowledge of a mystery into 'common words' and have lost our vision and the memory of the way to the hidden country to which our real selves belong. In our nostalgia we blame a multitude of causes for this century's failure to produce great drama, but we seldom reflect that one of the roots of our predicament is the denial of the poetic process, a denial that strangles the poet in our dramatists. Nowhere in dramatic technique is this more disastrous than in the technique of portraying character.

One of the odd corollaries of this false theorem is the application to the whole body of the traditional drama behind us of the conclusions from the practice and theories of the last hundred years. We accuse the great dramatists from Aeschylus downward (but principally Shakespeare, because more of us study him) of perpetrating an illusion in their presentation of character. The naturalists, in attempting to persuade us that a character in a work of art is a character in nature, lost touch with the deep, hidden wells of reality from which imagination

25

Shakespeare the Dramatist

draws its life, and the shallowness of their resultant rendering has at last forced itself upon our notice. And from this we unjustifiably conclude that 'character' in drama must always and necessarily be illusion, theatrical effect only, that will not bear investigating; and that the character-work of the great poetic dramatists, because it lacks even superficial likeness to everyday events, is more deeply guilty of illusion even than that of those naturalists. And so the serious investigation of the characters of Shakespeare's plays becomes at best a piece of venial day-dreaming, at worst a dangerous heresy. Whereas, in fact, it is the great poetic dramatists whose sure, unerring technique alone makes character revelation possible, because it alone finds anything to reveal, and the one thing that their presentation needs to assure us of this is investigation.[1]

I should like, with your permission, to illustrate what I mean at this point by reference to two specific passages. It must, of course, be understood that nothing less than the consideration of the total presentation of a character throughout a play (and preferably, of all the characters) could justly illustrate the technique of revelation. Extracts as brief as those which I must now use can do nothing more, even if they are passages of great significance, than illustrate the function of speech in a brief dialogue. What depends upon action, in so far as that can be distinguished from speech, is necessarily omitted and we lose further the cumulative power which the interrelation of action and speech gives to both and that further potent effect which the successive phases of the revelation derive from their place in the total action. But I am convinced that what is true of these passages is true one-hundredfold of the total effect of the play and that the distinction I am attempting to draw becomes more, not less, apparent as we pursue it further.

I choose for my first passage a short extract from the second Act of *Ghosts*, one of the few plays of Ibsen whose claim to the

[1] There follows, in the draft, a passage which was used, in a revised form, in 'Ibsen and Shakespeare as Dramatic Artists'. See below, p. 139.

The Mode of the Dramatist

title of tragedy can hardly be denied under any definition, ancient or modern. It is the passage in which Manders and Mrs Alving speak face to face after years of silence and strip away one by one the veils that have hidden their past. It is a scene charged with passion, the stored-up bitterness of fruitless sacrifice, and yet it is as lucid as a logical or legal analysis, because the speaker, a woman of fearless and powerful mind, has subjected these injuries, and the moral code that caused them, to a slow, pitiless, and scientific examination through long years of solitude. It arises with the perfect naturalness of a mountain peak from its massif, for these two lovers who for years have been enemies are confronted with a situation which suddenly releases the pent-up thinking of a lifetime.

MRS ALVING. Let me tell you what I mean. I'm timid and half-hearted because I can't get rid of the ghosts that haunt me.

MANDERS. What do you say haunts you?

MRS ALVING. Ghosts! When I heard Regina and Oswald in there, it was as though I saw ghosts before me. But I almost think we're all of us ghosts, Pastor Manders. It's not only what we have inherited from our father and mother that 'walks' in us. It's all sorts of dead ideas, old lifeless beliefs, and so forth. They have no vitality; but they cling to us all the same, and we can't get rid of them. Whenever I take up a newspaper I seem to see ghosts gliding between the lines. There must be ghosts all over the country, as thick as the sand of the sea. And then we're all of us so pitifully afraid of the light.

MANDERS. Ah! here we have the fruits of your reading! And pretty fruits they are, upon my word! Those horrible, revolutionary, free-thinking books!

MRS ALVING. You're mistaken, my dear Pastor. It was you yourself set me thinking. And I thank you for it with all my heart.

MANDERS. I?

MRS ALVING. Yes. When you forced me under the yoke you called 'Duty' and 'Obligation'; when you praised as right and proper what my whole soul rebelled against, as against something loathsome. It was then I began to look into the seams of your doctrine. I only meant to pick at a single knot; but when I'd got that undone, the whole thing ravelled out. And then I realized that it was all machine-sewn.

MANDERS (*softly, with emotion*). And was that the upshot of my life's hardest battle?

MRS ALVING. Call it, rather, your most pitiful defeat.

MANDERS. It was my greatest victory, Helen – the victory over myself.

MRS ALVING. It was a crime against us both.

MANDERS. When you went astray, and came to me crying, 'Here I am; take me!', I commanded you, saying – 'Woman, go home to your lawful husband.' Was that a crime?

MRS ALVING. Yes, I think so.

MANDERS. We two do not understand each other.

MRS ALVING. Not now, at any rate.

None of us would deny to this scene, thinking of it in its place in the drama, its cogency, the intensity of its passionate thought. It impresses us; almost it moves us; certainly it rivets our attention. Two minds are in conflict upon a moral issue. A life-history is revealed, lucidly, painfully; its case is pleaded before us, like a case in a court. We listen intently, we sympathize, as, step by step, actions are explained by motive and motive in its turn by freshly interpreted fact. For in this court we are the judge and the plaintiff pleads her own case before us in this reinterpretation of fact and motive. But there is a fatal limitation in this function of judge that is forced upon us. For what kind of revelation of character have we? And what kind of response does it call out in us? We should, of course, have no difficulty in describing the outstanding traits of the two people before us; there is no failure to define their characteristics. But what is there, in this clear self-analysis and self-defence, of the deeper movements of character, what sudden disclosure of the vast unexplored territories of the mind, seen suddenly as through parting mists, such as, in a single line of

The Mode of the Dramatist

Aeschylus, reveals to us a human soul akin to the unknown or
half-known soul within ourselves?

οὐδεὶς ἀκούει ταῦτα τῶν εὐδαιμόνων.
(Alas, none that is happy knows that word.)[1]

In that line Cassandra, at the crisis of her tragedy, discovers and
lets fall one of those great truths whose perception changes the
habit of a mind, transforms its reading of life. What communication have we, in the noble elucidation of Mrs Alving's
motive and behaviour, with the region of the spirit from which
such knowledge as Cassandra's comes? And yet can we really
be said to have tragic character when we are cut off from these
intimations, when we are restricted to the conscious, reasoning
operations of the mind, which are the best we can hope for in
a play in which the characters must perforce explain themselves
if they are to be known at all? And is this technique, the inevitable result of his commitment to naturalism, ultimately
worthy of the genius of Ibsen, however closely his architectural power interlocks the parts of the action, down to the
smallest detail, however strongly his passion, held prisoner
within that flawless and unbreakable design, throbs through the
hard, clear dialogue? 'Je ne reconnais plus l'auteur du *Misan-
thrope*'; we miss the poet of the fifth act of *Peer Gynt* and of
the death of John Gabriel Borkman.

But if we turn back to Shakespeare we meet a technique that
wastes no time or strength in trying to persuade us that a play
is not a play or that the words that lie before us on the
page are an exact reproduction of those of everyday life.
The great poetic dramatists are mercifully delivered from this
temptation by the traditional forms of their lines; no one has,
I believe (not even in the criticism of the last hundred years),
contended that the Elizabethans habitually spoke blank verse,
the citizens of Athens iambics, or the audiences of the Hôtel
de Bourgogne alexandrines. And, in this matter of dramatic

---

[1] *Ag.* 1303.

29

technique, to be committed in advance to a great traditional convention, even if it govern no more than the vehicle of speech,
is to be delivered from a host of misconceptions as to the relation between the truth (or reality) to be communicated and
the medium through which it is transmitted. If our characters
cannot speak the rhythms of everyday life, we are protected
against the assumption that they can be made to sound as if
they were living their outward lives before us. If we are guarded
thus against the temptation to present those actual, outward
lives as themselves an aspect of reality, we are free to use our
brief dramatic span to reveal the enduring, the universal, the
inward experience of man. But to do that, in so brief space, we
must use, boldly, another technique – a technique that is not
afraid of (has not indeed regarded) its unrealistic mode; a
technique that indicates character by touches, by silences, by
omissions, but by touches of such rare significance that their
presence in those silences evokes in our imagination an ever-
growing, living organism, a whole that is a character. To use
language thus to indicate and evoke character is not to practise
illusion, any more than do those few brief words in which the
mystic images a part of his experience and evokes a corresponding understanding in those who can receive them. In the
technique of revealing character in drama, it is, I repeat, the
only way to achieve a revelation of validity and scope.

MACBETH

Two Truths are told,
As happy Prologues to the swelling Act
Of the Imperiall Theame. I thanke you Gentlemen:
This supernaturall solliciting
Cannot be ill; cannot be good. If ill,
Why hath it giuen me earnest of successe,
Commencing in a Truth? I am *Thane* of Cawdor.
If good, why doe I yeeld to that suggestion,
Whose horrid Image doth vnfixe my Heire,

30

The Mode of the Dramatist

And make my seated Heart knock at my Ribbes,
Against the vse of Nature? Present Feares
Are lesse then horrible imaginings:
My Thought, whose Murther yet is but fantasticall,
Shakes so my single state of Man, that Function
Is smother'd in surmise, and nothing is,
But what is not.

The turmoil and mystery of man's unknown self is released
by this passage as great music releases it. It is a series of potent
images that drop like deep shafts into the hidden wells of man's
being to reach a strange and terrifying reality. If we were to
examine it word by word, each phrase, each image, each suggestion would serve to lead us into speculation, into knowledge
the total expression of which in explicit terms would demand
a volume of writing no less in extent than a whole play (supposing, which is clearly impossible, that such explication could
be conceived in dramatic form at all). For it works upon us not
through our judgement but by direct appeal to that vast,
hidden imaginative self which it alone can reach. In the whole
passage no sentence has the form of normal speech, except that
in which Macbeth breaks away for a moment from his preoccupation in the brief 'I thank you, Gentlemen'. We may ask
ourselves, 'What does this tell us of character?' And the answer
at first may seem to be 'Nothing', for such moments are the
meeting-grounds of passion and inchoate thought that overwhelm characteristics and resolve the individual man into the
eternal, the universal, the generic. It tells us little of those
superficial traits and characteristics by which we so readily sum
up character as it appears to offer itself in the everyday commerce of life and in the drama that attempts to work in terms
of that commerce. But there is, after all, ample time for such
indication of those features as we shall need in the play, by a
casual reference here and there, by the juxtaposition of speech
and action. What we have here is the deep working of half-
hidden and half-articulate motive such as, in ourselves and other

men, seems to overwhelm individuality, that 'drowning of the dykes', that 'perishing into reality' in which Yeats found the essential tragic experience. Yet, when we look more closely, whether it is at the 'character' Shakespeare has called Macbeth or at similar moments in our own experience, we know that this is not all; that in this evocation of mysterious forces, this exploration of unknown depths, the individuality is not utterly obliterated. Riding the torrent it cannot stem, it survives into a measure of choice, and what follows, in its action and thought, will have a power withheld in art or life from the 'character' that is rooted in its own consciousness. Put the limitless and 'still-breeding' implication of this brief indication of the hidden world of Macbeth's mind beside the limits that Ibsen, at the stage of *Ghosts*, deliberately sets to the definition of his problem, and dare we do otherwise than reverse the popular verdict of our day? It is the technique of Ibsen's four realistic plays, and more still that technique as practised by dramatists of lesser genius, which makes the presentation of character in drama an illusion. It is the evocative and non-realistic technique of Shakespeare and the poetic dramatists that leads us to reality. Indeed, as Blake said: 'Improvement makes straight roads, but crooked roads without improvement are roads of Genius.' Only by abandoning the apparent safeguards of verisimilitude can drama, especially in this branch of its technique, become the vehicle of the deepest-hidden truth. Ibsen's characters live the examined life commended by Plato: ὁ ἀνεξέταστος βίος οὐ βιωτὸς ἀνθρώπῳ;[1] but Shakespeare's art, like all great poetry, depends on another mode of being, commended in another place: 'Amen, amen dico vobis, nisi granum frumenti cadens in terram mortuum fuerit, ipsum solum manet; si autem mortuum fuerit, multum fructum affert', or the hidden life without safeguards which is the life of the mystics and of the great ideal poets.

We might very well have reached our conclusion as to the relative validity of these techniques by a different road, and I

[1] *Ap.* 38A.

32

The Mode of the Dramatist

shall attempt in the space that I have left to indicate this. Ibsen and Shakespeare, like all artists, faced the inexorable task of selection. Even the realist cannot escape this, but it is the dramatic realist's misfortune that he must often pretend to do so. We can watch Ibsen at work and see something of the magnificent sureness with which he selects and re-combines, of the architectural economy that doubles and trebles the significance of every part or fragment by the relating to it of every other. But life does not select, and the need to hide the fact that the artist does taxed to the uttermost even Ibsen's powers, while the verisimilitude of lesser dramatists broke down, even as verisimilitude, in the effort to appear to use only the actual when one aspect of that actual is precisely a mass of detail that could in no circumstances be used. And so the nature of the selection the dramatist makes becomes the governing factor in his presentation of truth, in character as in all other branches of technique. Nothing can save him from this law, and his peril is his glory. He will be aware (consciously or unconsciously – or both) of event and character as a continuous stream of what for brevity's sake we will call experience, and his task as an artist is to dip into that stream and draw from it, now here, now there, small quantities which can never, by the very nature of the artistic process, be more than a minute proportion of the whole, disconnected, isolated from each other, and to sacrifice the rest of that vast continuum which is the material of inner and outward experience. Nothing can save him from disastrous errors of omission and wrong emphasis that would give a lying picture of reality except that gift of divination which is genius and the hidden, fundamental, and mysterious operations of its power. If he trusts instead to the operation of the intellect working upon observation, however acute, of the surface of life, he cuts himself off from the sources of power and of illumination.

I have spoken so far of the method by which the dramatist may transmit his perception of reality in character, as in other branches of technique, but in doing so I have made two obvious

Shakespeare the Dramatist

assumptions: that there is a reality to transmit and that the great poet is one of the channels for its transmission. I do not want to end without indicating my meaning here, since the test of technical validity depends upon a relation between technique and content.

For the purposes of this argument, I will merely say that I take truth, which the great artist communicates, to be a part or parts of a complete and irreducible reality, such as might be discerned by an unerring and all-including intelligence, which some of us find it briefer and less cumbersome to call God. I consider further that the spiritual universe affords the means for the knowledge of this truth; that it is part of its nature to do so. I believe this knowledge to be possible under certain conditions to human faculties, to such faculties, for instance, as are possessed by the great poets and the great saints. I believe, that is to say, that in this continuum of experience, of which we have spoken, it is possible to either of them to discern certain significant elements, unnameable perhaps by either and for the artist certainly better undefined, which so work upon the imagination as to produce awareness of form, of the presence of intention, of the operation of underlying law. Provided, that is to say, that the poet has within his power the means of transmission (and it has been my object here to discuss one particular aspect of his choice of those means), he is capable of transmitting truth, and that truth is there to be communicated.

But the distinction between the presentation of character in terms of statement and its indication by means of the evocative technique remains within the province of dramatic aesthetics. Since, as we have demonstrated, the technique of statement cannot reveal so much or so profoundly as can the evocative technique, the method, even in the hands of Ibsen, is a hindrance to drama, and, so far, undramatic. It appears to present reality, only to provoke the accusation that 'character' in drama is an illusion. Whereas in fact, even with the realists, the illusion is all in the technique and the 'character' imagined (and in part

34

The Mode of the Dramatist

transmitted, despite the technique) is an aspect of imaginative truth. But in the great poetic dramatists, who proceed by evocation, there is, rightly understood, no attempt to present a likeness to the surface of character. Speeches, phrases, single words even, are all indications, leading the imagination on to awareness and comprehension for which the intelligence has no words, to comprehension of processes of emotion, of hitherto unperceived depths and complexities of character which the dramatist himself has discerned. The touch which disengages these is the ultimate test of the genuine dramatist; the dramatist's technique when it is supreme is wholly evocative. Free to work, then, in terms of their great, traditional evocative technique, and using only so much of surface resemblance (and a very little is in fact needed) as will serve to stimulate the twin sympathies of pity and fear, the great dramatists speak, through their characters, from the depths of their own poetic experience to the depths of man's nature. And their reward is that the 'characters' they create will speak for ever, or for so long as human imagination survives to hear them.

III

Shakespeare and the Dramatic Mode [1]

FOR NEARLY A CENTURY and a half now Shakespeare has been generally admitted to be one of the greatest of the world's dramatists and for nearly two hundred years certain of his readers have believed him the greatest of all. For in his mature work he seems to stand alone in fulness of achievement. This belief is undoubtedly due, in the first place, to his supreme possession of all the essential qualities or powers that belong to a great dramatist; the passion, the thought, and the sympathy with human experience that characterize the true dramatic imagination. And no other writer seems to have so full and unflawed possession of all these simultaneously. He stands supreme, not simply as the greatest writer using the dramatic form, but precisely because he is a dramatist. Being in all things the essential dramatist, his greatness is commensurate with the essentially dramatic quality in him; the quality constitutes the greatness. Or, to put it rather differently, it is precisely because he is more profoundly and more fully dramatic than any other that he is supreme.

If this is true, if it is the essential dramatist that is the essential Shakespeare, we may expect to find in his writing, as a part of the revelation of his powers, some correspondingly distinctive mode of dramatic expression; some way, that is, of transmitting his perceptions, something in his revealing of character or his articulation of structure which is distinctive precisely by reason of its service to dramatic ends. Here again, we should not expect

[1] Printed in *Neophilologus* (1952), pp. 104–12. Some passages, omitted from this article, have been restored from the typewritten copy.

to find him in sole possession of this secret, but we might discover that his continuous possession of it set him apart from all but a few of the greatest, and perhaps that the failure of others in respect of this peculiar artistic skill helped both to explain their relative failure as dramatists and to define, even more clearly, the wholly and supremely dramatic nature of Shakespeare's art.

The peculiar feature of his art that I have in mind, and that I venture to consider the distinctive mode in dramatic writing, is to be found in his way of revealing the profound movements of character or the hidden logic of event. His readers receive so nearly direct an impression of these that the immediacy, which is one source of the theatre's compelling power, is undimmed in the transmitting. We remain continuously immersed in the character's experience; we never cease to be Macbeth; we are never invited to observe him. This is in fact the essential difference between 'Guilty creatures sitting at a play' and those sitting at a sermon.

Many critics have, of course, been aware of Shakespeare's habit of writing from the depths and of a wholly different way of going to work on the part of certain other dramatists. In England, in the late eighteenth century, Lord Kames denounced the type of play in which description of experience was substituted for its revelation and, nearly simultaneously, Maurice Morgann gave us the unforgettable sentence, 'Shakespeare contrives to make secret impressions upon us'.

The difference depends, in the first instance, upon the depth to which the dramatist's perception has carried him, on his understanding of hidden motive and the hidden relations of events. But it is manifested in his power to make us in our turn aware of these hidden movements, by means, as Morgann puts it, of those 'secret impressions', whereby we come into imaginative possession of realities beyond the reach of our conscious understanding. And it is the faculty which enables some dramatists so to communicate to the imaginations of their audiences

37

Shakespeare the Dramatist

the truths learned from their own imaginative explorations, while still using only the medium of speech and action common to all drama, that distinguishes them in respect of mode. A poet's knowledge of man's experience and of the obscure movements of event that make up his destiny may be profound, but when he attempts to communicate this in a play he must so use those technical resources of speech and action, as to evoke in his audience an imaginative response at a depth corresponding to that of the imagined experience of his character. The transmission is necessarily made through the medium of words and actions, which themselves constitute the visible surface of life: this is a primary law of drama, since immediacy of impression is there a necessity. But in the greatest drama it is so made as to be simultaneously the clue to those hidden processes which the surface in no way necessarily resembles. All great poetry makes its communication at a level below the surface meaning of the words; depth speaks to depth in line after line of Wordsworth's greatest passages. But the dramatist, working only in terms of the speech and action of imagined characters, has a task of peculiar difficulty and a reward, if he surmounts it, of peculiar glory. At the summit of its achievement, as in the greatest plays of Shakespeare, of Aeschylus, of Sophocles, this art conveys at once the reality of depth and the immediacy of direct presentation.

And now appears the paradox we have already suggested, for the surface of life in most societies differs from its underlying cause more often than it resembles it, being, in fact, rather an indication of its presence than an exact reflection of its form. Thomas Hardy, in a poem called 'The Slow Nature', once isolated this simple truth with great clarity and with an analytical precision denied to the dramatist, who must not make his own comments. A countrywoman, in this poem, receives the news of her husband's sudden death with seeming apathy. The only thing that appears to concern her is that the house is not yet in order and the beds not yet made. The neighbour who breaks

38

the news is shocked at this evidence of an unfeeling heart, this preoccupation with unimportant details. But it was not an unfeeling heart that caused that first reaction; hers was a slow nature and the passage from inner experience to outward expression was a long and devious one. A fortnight later she began to droop and soon after she was dead herself. There had been no obvious evidence, in her first bewildered response, of the mortal shock that had already laid hold on her; the surface conduct utterly belied the truth that was later proved. Now, Hardy sets out explicitly this relationship between depth and surface; he isolates this particular sequence of cause and effect by making of it a brief work of art; he picks out, if not always for comment, at least for emphasis and for juxtaposition (which almost constitutes comment), the main points in his story. A dramatist can do few of these things, though he may know as well as Hardy that the story is true and that the recognition of such truth is essential to the understanding of human nature in life or in drama. But he is here at the heart of a paradox of dramatic art, compelled to reveal the unseen through the seen, which offers no dependable image of it and may even at times be in flat contradiction. He must, in a sense Polonius never intended, 'by indirections find directions out'; and his 'indirections', his 'assays of bias', are sometimes little less than the total content of the play. So at least it is with Shakespeare in the fulness of his powers: Cordelia's behaviour, in the first scene of *King Lear*, offers a surface utterly at variance with her deeplying motives; her knowledge of them is by no means as full as is Shakespeare's or even as ours must attempt to be. A modern dramatist, Pirandello, attempted to meet this paradox by demonstrating schematically the surprises that await his imaginary investigators as they proceed, with an orderliness seldom permitted to the average observer, to examine level below level of truth or reality, only to find a succession of contradictions, something, at each step, different from the appearance that had covered it. Each appearance, in such plays, is at once a fact in

Shakespeare the Dramatist

its own right and the sign of a deeper-lying fact which it mis-
represents while yet deriving from it. A long recession of such
reassessments is implied, each leading to another which appears
in turn to invalidate it, although Pirandello only analyses the
first few terms of the series. We know that neither life nor great
drama is as neat as this, but the truth to which Pirandello and
Hardy point us, which they in fact so precisely isolate for our
inspection, is of the first order of importance when we consider
the nature of drama and its relation to the multiform evidence
that it takes for its material.

The dramatist's mind, that is to say, and the drama he creates,
must move not merely in a two-dimensional world, cause and
effect, motive, action and reaction being enacted and observed
upon a single plane, but also in a bewildering series of planes,
each with its own related world of cause and result, each obscurely related with, yet different in kind and in form from,
those above and beneath. In this three-dimensional world, this
ocean of experience, he is guided by intuitions of depth and
distance; but he is bound, by the nature of dramatic art, to
reveal his perceptions in terms of the end-product of the process he has discerned, in terms of that efflorescence upon the
surface which is made up of the words and deeds of his characters. Only by so disposing these that, simultaneously with their
outward and recognizable surface forms, there are revealed also
the varying depths from which they took their origin, can he
hope to reveal also what he has divined, either of those depths
or of the mysterious relationship. Moreover, again because of
the nature of his art, he must, out of the great complexity even
of this surface take only a few fragmentary details, mere hints
and indications of the vast movements, currents and powers,
of the infinite variety that lies below, having, after all, for the
instrument of his expression, only the words contained in some
3000 verse lines.

This is why I have suggested that it is precisely in revealing
his apprehension of these relations, surface to surface, depth to

40

depth and each to all, that the dramatist discloses the measure at once of his spirit's capacity and of his strength as an artist. Unless he has transcendent capacity of soul, he cannot explore the ultimate depths the knowledge of which will alone give the stamp of verity to his expression. If he has not great strength as an artist, the tyranny of the dramatic form, even it may be of specific conventions in a specific age, will force him to misrepresent or pervert such reality as he has perceived. For the tragic dramatist, as for all major artists, the cost of this knowledge is no less than a descent into hell, and in this journey only the greatest travel far: they are with Dante and with Wordsworth, with Beethoven and with Michelangelo. But no imaginative artist can avoid some part of the experience and so all dramatists are committed to the attempt, whether they will or no.

It is evident, moreover, that, in the process whose nature I have attempted to indicate, there are many ways of failing. And it may be that, by turning aside for a moment to examine some of these, we may arrive at a clearer notion of what constitutes, in the work of Shakespeare and those nearest to him, what I have called the dramatic mode and learn something of the way by which he touches the imaginations of his readers.

In passages which represent the speech and conduct of people in moments of intense experience or in the grip of sudden crises, it is clearly laid upon the dramatist to reveal strong and it may be conflicting emotions. But since, as we have already noticed, certain dramatists attempt to do this by methods which are in essence undramatic, we may consider now a passage in which a dramatist, abandoning, as it seems to me, his function as a dramatist, sets one of his characters to speak, in a moment of emotional crisis, not as a human being doing or suffering, but as an onlooker describing the effects of an emotion. I am going to choose a passage from Corneille's *Polyeucte*, not because I think it representative of Corneille's art as a whole, but because his mode is often of this kind, in the last analysis an essentially undramatic kind, and because the passage, which could readily be paralleled in much European drama of the seventeenth and eighteenth centuries, is precisely what we need to make the extreme position clear. It comes from the first scene of the second act, in which Fabian meets Sévère to break to him the news that Pauline, his betrothed, has been forced during Sévère's absence to marry another man. The speech of Sévère which immediately follows the reception of Fabian's news is characteristic of what I mean by an undramatic mode, for Corneille's character gives us a lecture on his emotional condition – not a very good lecture, at that – instead of becoming the channel for its communication.

FABIAN

Je tremble à vous le dire; elle est . . .

SÉVÈRE

Quoi?

FABIAN

Mariée.

SÉVÈRE

Soutiens-moi, Fabian; ce coup de foudre est grand,
Et frappe d'autant plus, que plus il me surprend.

FABIAN

Seigneur, qu'est devenu ce généreux courage?

SÉVÈRE

La constance est ici d'un difficile usage;
De pareils déplaisirs accablent un grand coeur;
La vertu la plus mâle en perd tout vigeur;
Et quand d'un feu si beau les âmes sont éprises
La mort les trouble moins que de telles surprises.
Je ne suis plus a moi quand j'entends ce discours.
Pauline est mariée!

42

Shakespeare and the Dramatic Mode

Truly, of this and similar passages, we may say with Voiture 'On ne debite pas les lieux communs quand on est profondément affligé'. And truly, again, in Corneille's own medium of drama, Shakespeare will afford us the contrast. We all remember the third scene of the fourth act of *Macbeth*, in which Ross, who hates and bungles the task laid upon him, breaks to Macduff the news that his wife and children have been killed by order of Macbeth. We remember the young and as yet unfledged Malcolm playing a part somewhat like Fabian's in Corneille's play and endeavouring to rally Macduff's courage. But Macduff's reply, though it conveys a truth that is itself more profound and subtle than any of Sévère's abstract generalizations, comes in the language of drama, not of the lecture-hall. We overhear Macduff's mind, as it stumbles towards the realization, now seeming to grasp it entire, now faltering back into incredulity, then as suddenly meeting the shock of some fresh implication. The emotions themselves are tumultuous and entangled: grief, rage, the tenderest pity and self-reproach; the vivid colours interlace but do not mingle. This is the image of a mind as yet in chaos, not of the resultant that we shall find when the forces have come into equilibrium. (That comes where it belongs, at the end of the fifth act.) The duration of the chaos is brief, because this is the portrait of a man trained to action and decision, with the habit of a soldier and a commander; but while it lasts it is a vivid picture of the tumult of the soul. Macduff thinks aloud and intersperses his half-unconsciously uttered thoughts with questions that now leap ahead, now double back over the track he has covered: he no more knows what is happening to him than a man with concussion and he is no condition to explain it to the audience or to anyone else. He tells us nothing, but he reveals everything.

Now if we look back again at Sévère, we realize afresh how incredibly prompt is his diagnosis of his own state of mind. The blow has barely fallen when he is in full command, if not of his emotions, at least of their explanation. With one step he

43

Shakespeare the Dramatist

becomes an onlooker, a commentator, instead of a man taken in the toils of an experience. There is half a line of genuine dramatic speech and then lucid exposition. It is magnificent, but it is not drama.

Nor is the speech of Félix to Albin in the fifth scene of the third act dramatic, in the sense here implied. Beginning with the pronouncement, 'On ne sait pas les maux dont mon coeur est atteint', it proceeds rapidly to rectify the deficiency through some seventeen lines of analytical description. There is no revelation there; we do not accompany the mind of Félix upon a journey. Still less are we aware, as we often are in the speech of Shakespeare's characters, of looking into a further depth of experience below that the character himself perceives. We listen with respectful interest to a lecture on a state of mind delivered by the patient himself; but our thoughts stray to the prayer of Claudius in *Hamlet*, or to Angelo's tormented communion with his soul.

FÉLIX

On ne sait pas les maux dont mon coeur est atteint;
De pensers sur pensers mon âme est agitée,
De soucis sur soucis elle est inquiétée;
Je sens l'amour, la haine, et la crainte, et l'espoir,
La joie et la douleur tour-à-tour l'émouvoir;
J'entre en des sentiments qui ne sont pas croyables;
J'en ai de violents, j'en ai de pitoyables;
J'en ai de généreux qui n'oseraient agir:
J'en ai même de bas, et qui me font rougir.
J'aime ce malheureux que j'ai choisi pour gendre,
Je hais l'aveugle erreur qui le vient de surprendre;
Je déplore sa perte, et, le voulant sauver,
J'ai la gloire des dieux ensemble à conserver;
Je redoute leur foudre, et celui de Décie;
Il y va de ma charge, il y va de ma vie.
Ainsi tantôt pour lui je m'expose au trépas,
Et tantôt je le perds pour ne me perdre pas.

44

Shakespeare and the Dramatic Mode

In this speech the expository manner is indeed more nearly justified, for its subject is a debate in the mind and not the reception of a sudden and overwhelming shock. But the soliloquy of debate has its own laws in drama and though these are of ample scope, there is a clear distinction between the enunciation of conclusions and the revelation of exploration and discovery, themselves accompanied by profound emotion. This is clear when we pass from Félix's speech to such a soliloquy as that of Angelo at the beginning of the fourth scene of the second act of *Measure for Measure*. He too might claim justifiably that no one can gauge the misery of his soul, but the difference is that, in Angelo's case, he cannot understand it himself and that a large part of our experience in reading his speech is precisely our experience of his own dismay:

> When I would pray, and think, I thinke, and pray
> To seuerall subiects: heauen hath my empty words,
> Whilst my Inuention, hearing not my Tongue,
> Anchors on *Isabell*: heauen in my mouth,
> As if I did but onely chew his name,
> And in my heart the strong and swelling euill
> Of my conception: the state whereon I studied
> Is like a good thing, being often read
> Growne sere, and tedious: yea, my Grauitie
> Wherein (let no man heare me) I take pride,
> Could I, with boote, change for an idle plume
> Which the ayre beats for vaine: oh place, oh forme,
> How often dost thou with thy case, thy habit
> Wrench awe from fooles, and tye the wiser soules
> To thy false seeming? Blood, thou art blood,
> Let's write good Angell on the Deuills horne,
> 'Tis not the Deuills Crest:

Many kinds of technique intermediate between the undramatic and the wholly dramatic may obviously be found. In some, as in Dryden's best plays, a mixture of expository with evocative speech takes us a step nearer to the world of great poetic drama whose mode is wholly evocative. More subtly, in others, as in Corneille's *Le Cid*, the nature or habit of the characters goes part-way to justify their behaviour. Just as, in Ibsen's *Brand*, we recognize Brand's long, self-examining soliloquies as a process habitual to that mind and meet with sympathy the evident faithfulness of the expression, so, in Corneille's *Le Cid*, debates on points of principle come the nearer to dramatic revelation, simply because the characters so evidently have the habit of them. They are educated to constant conflict between their primal impulses and a military code of honour, noble in itself and so passionately held. Such men do not stop to think, because they know their responses by heart; they have been trained to expect conflicts between their code and their passions and so meet an onslaught on their emotions as a probblem in dynamics: they simply balance the forces and arrive at the resolution without doubt or undue dismay. Corneille is justified here, as Ibsen is later, and for the same kind of reason. His characters speak eloquently, like Brand, because, like Brand, they are on familiar ground. 'L'honneur est un devoir'; and they are accustomed to apply their minds vigorously to balancing the claims of opposing duties.

D. RODRIGUE

L'honneur vous en est dû, je ne pouvais pas moins,
Etant sorti de vous et nourri par vos soins.
Je m'en tiens trop heureux, et mon âme est ravie
Que mon coup d'essai plaise à qui je dois la vie;
Mais parmi vos plaisirs ne soyez point jaloux
Si je m'ose à mon tour satisfaire après vous.
Souffrez qu'en liberté mon désespoir éclate;
Assez et trop longtemps votre discours le flatte.
Je ne me repens point de vous avoir servi;
Mais rendez-moi le bien que ce coup m'a ravi.
Mon bras, pour vous venger, armé contre ma flamme,
Par ce coup glorieux m'a privé de mon âme;
Ne me dites plus rien; pour vous j'ai tout perdu;
Ce que je vous devais, je vous l'ai bien rendu.

Shakespeare and the Dramatic Mode

D. DIEGUE

Porte, porte plus haut le fruit de ta victoire:
Je t'ai donné la vie, et tu me rends ma gloire;
Et d'autant que l'honneur m'est plus cher que le jour,
D'autant plus maintenant je te dois de retour.
Mais d'un coeur magnanime éloigne ces faiblesses;
Nous n'avons qu'un honneur, il est tant de maîtresses!
L'amour n'est qu'un plaisir, l'honneur est un devoir.

Out of this Corneille makes something vivid that reminds us of Hotspur's 'easie leap, To plucke bright Honor from the pale-fac'd Moone'. Something, indeed, is revealed in this high state of excitement, brilliant with passion and torment and the high vitality of youth. But the evidence of the play as a whole belies the evidence of some single noble speeches of Rodrigue or of Chimène. Rodrigue is not Hotspur, because he is immaculate; and this is only another way of saying that Corneille allows us no glimpses of the confused or imperfect human being that Shakespeare ever and again suffers his Hotspur to disclose. And this means that he is in fact denying to us that communication with the depths of the character without which a play may be a brilliant effect of balanced stresses and forces, but will not be drama. The oratory of the pulpit or of the senate-house is not the speech of the theatre when that is in intimate relation with the profound activity of the poetic imagination.

But rather than Hotspur, we may choose another soldier to put beside those of *Le Cid*; a man as valiant, as deeply imbued with an honourable and aristocratic code; a man caught, as Rodrigue is here, between two conflicting duties, called upon to balance two rival claims within the code; a man less eloquent than Rodrigue, except in the language of his specialized, chivalric code, but no less vehement and as glorious in achievement. Does Shakespeare, bringing before us a situation not utterly unlike those in some of Corneille's plays and a group of characters raised in traditions not wholly unlike those of Corneille's

47

soldiers, afford us any further insight into the depths beneath
such surfaces?

Let us look for a moment at the third scene of the fifth act
of *Coriolanus*. Coriolanus, outlawed by the Roman mob, has
gone over to the enemy camp and is leading the Volscians to
the gates of Rome. He has bound himself by oath to the
Volscians and so his honour as a soldier is engaged to them, and
not to his country which had rewarded his services with
banishment. But the headlong career of his passion for revenge
is checked by the arrival of his mother, wife, and child and by
the sudden uprising of another group of emotions which
Volumnia deliberately brings to life again.

CORIOLANUS

My wife comes formost, then the honour'd mould
Wherein this Trunke was fram'd, and in her hand
The Grandchilde to her blood. But out affection,
All bond and priuiledge of Nature breake;
Let it be Vertuous to be Obstinate.
What is that Curt'sie worth? Or those Doues eyes,
Which can make Gods forsworne? I melt, and am not
Of stronger earth than others: my Mother bowes,
As if Olympus to a Mole-hill should
In supplication Nod: and my yong Boy
Hath an Aspect of intercession, which
Great Nature cries, Deny not. Let the Volces
Plough Rome, and harrow Italy, Ile neuer
Be such a Gosling to obey instinct; but stand
As if a man were Author of himself,
And knew no other kin.

VIRGILIA

My Lord and Husband.

CORIOLANUS

These eyes are not the same I wore in Rome.

Shakespeare and the Dramatic Mode

VIRGILIA

The sorrow that deliuers vs thus chang'd,
Makes you thinke so.

CORIOLANUS

Like a dull Actor now,
I haue forgot my part, and I am out,
Euen to a full Disgrace. Best of my Flesh,
Forgiue my Tyranny: but do not say,
For that forgiue our Romanes. O a kisse
Long as my Exile, sweet as my Reuenge!
Now by the iealous Queene of Heauen, that kisse
I carried from thee deare; and my true Lippe
Hath Virgin'd it ere since. You Gods, I prate,
And the most noble Mother of the world
Leaue vnsaluted: Sinke my knee i'th'earth,
Of thy deepe duty, more impression shew
Then that of common Sonnes. . . .

O Mother, Mother!
What haue you done? Behold, the Heauens do ope,
The Gods looke downe, and this vnnaturall Scene
They laugh at. Oh my Mother, Mother: Oh!
You haue wonne a happy Victory to Rome.
But for your Sonne, beleeue it: Oh beleeue it,
Most dangerously you haue with him preuail'd,
If not most mortall to him. But let it come:
Auffidius, though I cannot make true Warres,
Ile frame conuenient peace. Now good *Auffidius*,
Were you in my steed, would you haue heard
A Mother lesse? or granted lesse, *Auffidius*?

AUFIDIUS

I was mou'd withall.

E   49

CORIOLANUS

I dare be sworne you were:
And sir, it is no little thing to make
Mine eyes to sweat compassion. But (good sir)
What peace you'l make, aduise me: For my part,
Ile not to Rome, Ile backe with you, and pray you
Stand to me in this cause. Oh Mother! Wife!

AUFIDIUS (*aside*)

I am glad thou hast set thy mercy and thy Honor
At difference in thee: Out of that Ile worke
My selfe a former Fortune.

CORIOLANUS

I, by and by;
But we will drinke together: And you shall beare
A better witnesse backe then words, which we
On like conditions, will haue Counter-seal'd.
Come enter with vs: Ladies you deserue
To haue a Temple built you: All the Swords
In Italy, and her Confederate Armes
Could not haue made this peace.

Now here is a man analysing his own feelings, and doing it
for the most part with the incompetence of people who mis-
trust the process even while indulging in it; here is seemingly
description instead of revelation; here apparently is what Lord
Kames condemns in the tragedies of his age, 'a cold description
in the language of a bystander', a thing no more excusable in
Coriolanus than in Sévère or Félix, Almanzor or Rodrigue.
Furthermore, the restless brilliance of Rodrigue's speech is
wanting. But is this in fact the thing that seizes our imaginations? We have read or watched the play, we have already been
immersed during four acts and a half in the passions of Coriolanus and the entanglement of those passions in the fortunes of
Rome and of the Volscians. We no longer accept as the poet's

intimation of the truth what Coriolanus says about himself. But we are profoundly concerned with the fact that he says it. Self-explanation in Coriolanus is not a dramatist's clumsy substitute for revelation; it is the profound and tragic disclosure of the nature of a man who 'hath euer but slenderly knowne himselfe'. This underlying nature, deep buried and hidden more successfully from himself even than from those who surround him, has been gradually communicating itself to us by 'secret impressions' throughout the play. We may not at this point know precisely what that nature is, perhaps we never apprehend it clearly; but we know by now that it is utterly unlike what he himself here believes it to be. He has been subjected, under terrific pressure, to a heroic ideal as dangerously divorced from normal humanity as that high code upon which Rodrigue was nourished. But Shakespeare's figure is not, like Corneille's, the walking embodiment of a code; he is a recognizable human being bearing about him evidences of the cost of such a process. He speaks a conventional language as fluently as does Rodrigue, but the image of himself that he sees and proclaims is a vast, inhuman thing:

> Like to a lonely Dragon, that his Fenne
> Makes fear'd, and talk'd of more then seene . . .
> Ile neuer
> Be such a Gosling to obey instinct; but stand
> As if a man were Author of himself,
> And knew no other kin.

The inflation of his imagery is there to point the way to our discovery, and if the imagery failed (which it could not) the rhythm of the lines would do the work. Coriolanus explains himself. Yes: and the explanation is a figment so fantastic that its presence testifies, as nothing else could do, to the tumult of a soul denied its primal rights of sane and normal growth.

In this scene, where the potency of the conflicting forces is greater than in any other, some faint shadow of the truth seems

about to reach him, like intimations in a dream. The imagery of
acting runs through the scene,

> Like a dull Actor now,
> I haue forgot my part . . .

and not least of the terrible ironies in this scene is the fact that
he speaks such lines half-jestingly; lines that contain the clue to
the tragedy of his spirit.

This, briefly, is the difference between the undramatic technique of which Lord Kames complained and the true dramatic
mode. Never is the difference more clearly illuminated than
when a genuine dramatist, while serving his own dramatic
purposes, shows that he too perceives it.

Finally, we may consider the third scene of the first act of
Hamlet, in which Shakespeare's way of disclosing the movements of a mind and the nature of a character is finely and
subtly revealed, the scene in which Ophelia's brief speeches
explain so little of what is happening beneath the surface of
her mind that a dramatist of the expository school would
doubtless have given her long passages of expostulation, of
distress, of self-analysis, passages that would have been utterly
foreign to the impression Shakespeare so surely and so 'secretly'
makes upon us.

POLONIUS

What ist *Ophelia* he hath said to you?

OPHELIA

So please you, somthing touching the Lord *Hamlet*.

POLONIUS

Marry, well bethought:
Tis told me he hath very oft of late
Giuen priuate time to you; and you your selfe
Haue of your audience beene most free and bounteous.
If it be so, as so tis put on me;

Shakespeare and the Dramatic Mode

And that in way of caution: I must tell you,
You doe not vnderstand your selfe so cleerely,
As it behoues my Daughter, and your Honour.
What is betweene you, giue me vp the truth?

OPHELIA

He hath my Lord of late, made many tenders
Of his affection to me.

POLONIUS

Affection, puh. You speake like a greene Girle,
Vnsifted in such perillous Circumstance.
Doe you beleeue his tenders, as you call them?

OPHELIA

I do not know, my Lord, what I should thinke.

POLONIUS

Marry Ile teach you; thinke your selfe a Baby,
That you haue tane his tenders for true pay,
Which are not sterling. Tender your selfe more dearly;
Or not to crack the winde of the poore Phrase,
Running it thus, you'l tender me a foole.

OPHELIA

My Lord, he hath importun'd me with loue,
In honourable fashion.

POLONIUS

I, fashion you may call it, go too, go too.

OPHELIA

And hath giuen countenance to his speech, my Lord,
With almost all the holy vowes of Heauen.

53

Shakespeare the Dramatist

POLONIUS

I, Springes to catch Woodcocks. I doe know
When the Bloud burnes, how Prodigall the Soule
Giues the tongue vowes: these blazes, Daughter,
Giuing more light then heate; extinct in both,
Euen in their promise, as it is a making;
You must not take for fire. From this time Daughter,
Be somewhat scanter of your Maiden presence;
Set your entreatments at a higher rate,
Then a command to parley. For Lord *Hamlet*,
Beleeue so much of him, that he is young,
And with a larger tether may he walke,
Then may be giuen you. In few, *Ophelia*,
Doe not beleeue his vowes; for they are Broakers,
Not of that dye, which their Inuestments show:
But meere implorators of vnholy Sutes,
Breathing like sanctified and pious bawds,
The better to beguile. This is for all:
I would not, in plaine tearmes, from this time forth,
Have you so slander any moment leisure,
As to giue words or talke with the Lord *Hamlet*:
Looke too't, I charge you; come your wayes.

OPHELIA

I shall obey my Lord.

Now here, taken as it stands, we seem to see the portrait of
a submissive and rather characterless young girl; what was once
called an 'unformed character'; a being without vivid interests
or enjoyment, strong or eager impulses; content to do as she
is told in lazy dependence upon the wills and plans of those in
authority. We notice that Shakespeare gives Ophelia only six
speeches, none of them more than two lines in length; in all,
seven lines-and-a-half, as against a total of forty-eight in the
whole dialogue. The first two are plain and obedient replies to
her father's questions, the third is the simple confession, 'I do
not know, my lord, what I should think', the next two, faint

54

Shakespeare and the Dramatic Mode

attempts at justification, immediately quashed by Polonius's long and vigorous exhortation to discretion, and the last, a half-line of complete acceptance. Whatever she feels or fancies she feels about Hamlet is apparently removed from her mind as easily as chalk is rubbed off a blackboard. Jane Austen, we may remember, once made a full-length study of just such a soft and compliant character in Harriet Smith in *Emma*; Harriet obediently falls in love and out of love, makes friends and gives up, as Emma directs her. Such it would seem is the account of herself that Ophelia gives us in this scene; such are her words as they meet us on the surface.

But what relation does this bear to what is going on in her mind? Either the one we have already suggested, in which the brief speeches, with their prim, conventional phrasing, do in fact mirror faithfully the movements of soul from which they derive, or a relationship of contradiction and concealment. Perhaps we should suspect, beneath the formal statements, some conflict or confusion, less tumultuous than that to which the language of such a character as Coriolanus would point us, but not less fatally at odds with demeanour of the surface.

If we look back to the beginning of this scene, we find Ophelia alone with her brother, bidding him farewell. There is evidently some genuine affection between them; Laertes' grief in the later part of the play, even if it is too voluble for depth, is sincere in its kind. And so Ophelia is frank with him; gay, almost talkative, showing some eagerness of apprehension and some good sense. She accepts his lesson on self-control and the problems of public life soberly but without signs of distress. She calls it 'this good lesson', which on the whole it is, being in that respect utterly unlike the cheap and cynical shrewdness which Polonius recommends to each of his children in turn. Laertes sees Hamlet's position with sympathy and respect; he touches the situation with more profundity and generosity than his father – though perhaps it would be hard for any man to do so with less. And Ophelia recognizes a certain wisdom

55

in him and responds with frankness and a touch of genuine maturity. Already, we may observe, she 'has heard there are tricks in the world', though the conventional imagery of her references here, while she is still sane, contrasts sharply with the directness of this actual phrase, spoken later, in her madness, and shows her knowledge to be as yet but general and theoretical.

I have dwelt upon this short introductory passage, because it is the only one in which we see Ophelia as she was before the action of the tragedy engulfed her and because the sudden contrast of her gay but sane little conversation with her brother is in strong contrast with what immediately follows. She next listens to Polonius's advice to Laertes, that shrewd advocacy of ungenerous reserves and skilful façades, with its absurd and flat contradictions to its own cautions, and immediately upon this follows the dialogue in which Polonius applies his policy to the case of his younger child.

Something, it would seem, then chills her suddenly. It may be the respect due to her father, with whom she is not on as familiar terms as with Laertes or as many of Shakespeare's daughters are with their fathers. It may be an inarticulate, undefined, but none the less profound recoil from Polonius's coarse-grained, rule-of-thumb estimates of human motive, in conflict not only with the deference habitually paid to him as her guide, but with the deeper intimations of her own instinctive recognition of Hamlet's nature. All this, and perhaps some dim awareness that Laertes' going has robbed her of the only sympathetic counsellor she has known, are undoubtedly at work in her. It is enough that Shakespeare, through the intimations of the first part of the scene, has given us impressions which determine in us at unawares our hidden responses to her subsequent speech. Knowing also, in fact, what follows, the madness which is to testify to deep and inarticulate emotions, to the pressure upon her of forces whose values she cannot estimate and the conflict of faiths which she cannot share or express, we no longer have warrant for believing her indifferent or untouched. True, she is no Juliet whose inner confidence in the rightness of her passion makes her way straight. She is no Helena whose intellectual clarity determines and assesses her conduct. She lacks the native endowments of these, but she does not lack depth. Moreover, by ironic cruelty of circumstance, she is isolated with her own inexperience as neither of these more active natures was. Here is no friar to countenance and abet a secret marriage, no Countess of Rousillon to sympathize and support.

Bringing back then to the passage before us this legitimate knowledge from earlier and later scenes in the play, we see her moving in bewilderment through this dialogue, which now takes on the highest significance as the beginning of the process that is to lead her to madness and death. Now the colourless speeches begin to yield evidence of something moving beneath the surface, something agonized, bewildered, utterly at variance with their prim and meaningless form. Step by step, through the faint and easily strangled protests, to the final, numbed acquiescence that follows her long silence, we trace the process of a mind on whom the gates of fear and ignorance are closing until in truth it 'cannot tell' what it 'should think'.

Here then, again, as Morgann demonstrated in his analysis of Shakespeare's method with Falstaff, is a world of 'secret impressions' contradicting the surface evidence of words and actions, yet only to be discerned through what that surface can disclose, and each, both surface and hidden depth, derives a tragic and ironic meaning from the relationship between the two. Here, as throughout the plays, is the true dramatic mode, in which utterance proper to human reactions as it would appear in life itself, is yet, by the height of dramatic art, induced to reveal what lies beneath, as life itself often refuses to reveal it.

Every play of his maturity will reveal the same way of going to work, whether Lear is talking to the Fool in the fifth scene of the first act, or Lady Macbeth to Macbeth after the banquet.

It is most frequent in the tragedies and in them most potent in moments of high spiritual tension, precisely such moments as most often fail in the work of dramatists who attempt the technically easier but ultimately fatal method of laying upon their characters the responsibility of describing to us what their circumstances or condition would never permit them to perceive.

In one passage, and I think in one only, does Shakespeare show us the underside of this pattern, suffering us thereby to recognize at once the source from which each utterance is derived. We dare not say, even here, of what kind the connections are or by what process the spoken words derive from the hidden depths, but we come nearer to it than in any other passage. In the first scene of the fifth act of *Macbeth*, Lady Macbeth, speaking aloud though asleep, reveals through this special medium, the turmoil of soul of which only a bare hint had been given earlier. And there is not a word in her speeches which cannot be traced to an earlier moment in the play or found to be implicit in the action, a moment which, when it occurred, was met with a demeanour as firm, as clear and as effective as this is haunted and tormented. The existence of this scene is not necessary to our perception of the nature of Shakespeare's mode, but its presence should have left no doubt in our minds of the fact that that mode is an essential part of his art. And it is perhaps permissible to infer that not only is it essential to Shakespeare's art, but that it is itself the distinctive mode of all supreme drama.

We suggested at the end of Chapter II that the habit of identifying himself with every character wholly and simultaneously was closely related to the dramatist's use of an evocative and essentially dramatic mode. For only if he maintains that sympathy with all his characters, and with all of them simultaneously, does he so know them, in silence as in speech, in the intervals between events as in contributory action, as to know in each the image of a living creature and to know it far beyond the purposes for which the surface of the play uses it. But this knowledge must be communicated to the reader and audience, or at least potentially communicated, to the limit of their powers of reception. And no art, let alone the brief art of drama, could make this communication in explicit terms or in words whose function was no more than their connotation. Only the technique of evocation, with its 'generation of still-breeding thoughts' will allow this. Only the secret impressions at work in the imagination will serve the genuine dramatist for full communication.

IV

Coriolanus [1]

IN THE PLAYS OF his maturity, Shakespeare reveals by secret impressions the underlying natures of his characters, so that, with the knowledge thus conveyed to us, we redress at unawares the balance of evidence given not only by those characters but by other parts of the play. Many of those in which this process can be clearly discerned are minor or subordinate figures, but a few are co-partners with the greatest [2] and it is found to some degree in all. Of none can we say with certainty that we know them until we have taken into account the hidden evidence thus disclosed, and it is probable that our unconscious awareness of every character is influenced by it. But in one play at least Shakespeare seems to determine by this mode our apprehension of the central figure itself; and this so modifies the total effect of the play, as to re-colour our interpretation of nearly every aspect. No detailed analysis of such a character can be attempted within the limits of this volume, but some indications may be given of the process by which unconscious knowledge finds its way into our imaginations.

The character I have in mind is Coriolanus, one that we have already glanced at; [3] and the discrepancy between speech and fact, a certain conflict between the character's professions and

[1] This chapter was read at the Conference of the International Association of University Professors of English at Cambridge, August 1956. A summary appears in the Proceedings of the Conference.

[2] Such is the figure of Falstaff in which Maurice Morgann first discerned this method at work.

[3] See above, pp. 48–52.

60

Coriolanus

his actions may prompt us to look further into the mind from which both, though seemingly incompatible, derive. And this in turn may lead to successive readings that reveal depth below depth in his nature, re-interpreting the surface for us and modifying our first inferences from it.[1]

With the character of Coriolanus we observe first the strife and turmoil created by his passions on the world around him, shaking the State of Rome and bringing him to destruction, then the presence of bitter conflict in his own mind. From this point onward we are guided, I think, by deeper-lying and less evident indications of motive, until we reach a point where we depend wholly upon 'secret impressions' for the final interpretation. When we have reached this, we begin to travel backwards, in reascending order, as it were, to the surface which we first observed and to reconsider these earlier and it may be mistaken conclusions in the light of that final discovery.

Our first impression of Coriolanus in the first three acts of the play is familiar to all Shakespeare's readers and on this there may be little disagreement. He is a man still young[2] and of evident military genius, as brave and brilliant in battle as Hotspur, with powers of leadership in the field and a grasp of strategy akin to that of Henry V; a man whose valour and heroic wrath inspire men to follow him and carry them to

[1] The likelihood of an ultimate contradiction of his earlier judgement is sometimes suggested thus to the interpreter by the presence of conflict in and about the character, while sometimes it is conveyed rather by an uneasiness of mind recognized by the character himself but provoking no outward conflict. Sometimes, it may be, the contradiction offered to the surface and its evidence is so slight as to pass almost unobserved, as with the characters of Henry IV, Henry V, Volumnia and others.

[2] Coriolanus won his first campaign at the age of sixteen, like the historical Edward III, and had thus had time for much experience of war without becoming middle-aged by the time of the play. This makes Aufidius's taunt at the end – 'boy' – something that may justly infuriate and not a piece of mere gutter-snipe rudeness.

victory.[1] As a statesman, he shows in an emergency the same grasp of the essential factors; he is a clear and pitiless judge of the plebeians and a shrewd and fearless prophet of the immediate future. His impatient scorn of the people's cowardice and treachery, of the contemptible custom of vote-begging (accepted even by his fellow patricians), though fierce and heedless, is also of a heroic mould. He is a man of equally strong attachments within his own class, to his fellow generals Cominius, Menenius, and Titus Lartius, to his wife and above all to his mother; a sincere man, hating flattery, with an irritable dislike of praise, even when he has fairly earned it. These are the elements of a noble character and he reveals them clearly in action and eloquently in speech. On immediate political issues he is as sound a judge as on the conduct of a campaign; great intelligence as well as firm definition of thought shine through the courage and vigour of his speech.[2] His military genius (and, within these limits, his statesmanship) exceed the others' as his imagination surpasses theirs. In these two domains he appears to achieve full and untrammelled expression; passion and thought are in triumphant union. And the fruits of this may be seen in the liberal frankness of his manner during the first three acts to his fellow-generals and to Menenius; this is a man in at least momentary harmony with his immediate world.[3] If we accept this reading, his fall results directly from behaviour of a piece with what he has already shown us, from his intolerant, unsympathetic and heroically undiplomatic treatment of the insolent Roman mob. But after his fall the balance of his nature seems to change, and though some change might follow naturally upon the shock of his banishment, it is not altogether easy to interpret this as a direct development from his earlier behaviour. Darker moods and purposes than we or his fellows

[1] I. iv. 30 seq. I. vi. 66 seq.   [2] III. i. 37–40, 92, 104–11, 124–38, *141–60*.

[3] Never is this modest magnanimity more clearly revealed than in the scene during the consular campaign where he puzzles in simple bewilderment over his mother's disapproval of his conduct (III. ii. 7–16).

had suspected in him take possession and lead to his unnatural alliance with the Volscians, his vengeful attack on Rome and so to his death.

Thus already, in the reading these brief indications suggest, we find ourselves troubled by a seeming hiatus[1] at this point in the play. The haughty, heroic, and magnanimous patrician of the earlier acts is transformed into a vengeful soldier of fortune. The man who could not stay to hear his nothing monstered now sees himself as a lonely dragon whom his fen makes feared and talked of, and he who could not speak mildly to save his consulship flatters Aufidius's fellow-officers to win control of a war of vengeance.

And so a second impression begins to modify our first, though still drawn from the evidence of character and conduct revealed by the outward action of the play. For in seeking, as we must, to reconcile these two contradictory phases of conduct, to trace them to a common root in character, we have in fact already assumed the second to be inherent in the first. And so we begin to look for indications, for flaws that may be no more than faint inconsistencies; but that points us back or forward to the presence of something hitherto unnoticed in his nature, secretly at work, it may be, upon his experience, transforming it to something whose effects are incalculable to him, to us, and to his Roman world. One of the most evident of these flaws is the hyper-sensitive modesty of the early acts, churlish and ungrateful sometimes in its repudiation of praise that was in part at least kindly and courteous.[2] It is, as we have already noticed, in flat contradiction to his growing preoccupation, towards the end of the play, with the effect he is producing on other people and so belongs, presumably, to a part of his nature later submerged by the crucial act of treachery. But, more important than this, it is also hard to reconcile with our first impression, that of a man in full and glorious exercise of his power as a soldier, a confident man who, though vehement

[1] Menenius perceives this too (IV. vi. 72–4). [2] I. ix. 36–40, 40–53.

63

and irascible, yet expresses his political vision with full and satisfying vigour, a man secure in his close, affectionate relations with his friends and the members of his household. Beneath the confidence and the security, then, we recognize disharmony. And we ask from what it derives.

This leads us to consider other passages in the play, where openly declared difference of principle and conviction breaks out in the scenes in which Volumnia and the patricians force Coriolanus to conciliate the Roman mob he has defied.[1] This might be no more than a clash between two positive natures, each equally confident and secure in its own convictions, but that, as we observe, the divergence proves wider than Volumnia had supposed and its disclosure takes her by surprise. And we recall, too, an earlier moment of insistence on her part and uneasy acquiescence on his, where we are momentarily aware of something in him that she has not recognized. 'My mother, Who has a charter to extol her blood, When she does praise me grieves me.'[2] This is not idle talk; it reveals a deep division of idea, even an unrecognized division of ideals. Comparing the two passages, we recall what we have learnt of Volumnia's influence over Coriolanus, of her heroic ambition which has moulded his character and career.[3] We have been seeking to reconcile two contradictory phases of conduct in Coriolanus and have been led to assume the presence of division in his own mind. Now this assumption, at first suggested by that exaggerated sensitiveness, ungracious, ill-proportioned and at odds with his customary mood, is confirmed by the passages between him and Volumnia, which reveal not only the unexpected depth and inwardness of the division between them, but a like unformulated division in the mind of Coriolanus himself. For Coriolanus has been moulded in the ideals of his world (epitomized in his mother's) and though much in him has given them a willing response, we begin to question now whether they have been entirely of his own initiating, and whether they

[1] III. ii, especially 16–20.   [2] I. ix. 13–15.   [3] I. iii, etc.

Coriolanus

have in fact satisfied the whole of him. If his conduct, first in little, perplexing details of behaviour and finally in a great and catastrophic revolution, has pointed to a civil war within the mind of Coriolanus and if his mother's bearing and his relation to her has suggested a sufficient cause for this, can we go further and say that Shakespeare has revealed to us something of the nature of this war and of the conflicting elements involved, by further hints, in single phrases it may be, in momentary betrayals of something invisible and unknown to the speaker himself? For this would, if true, lead us to reconsider our earlier conclusions with the help of these impressions and so perhaps to come nearer to understanding what lies below the contradictions that first prompted our inquiry.

What picture does Shakespeare give us of this Roman civilization with which Coriolanus is in these passages at odds, which has yet shaped his habits, which has been his world and his devotion, to which his mother has dedicated him and to which he has offered his genius in eager and triumphant service? We might set aside the part played by the mob (which, to his fellow-patricians as to him, is hardly Rome at all and certainly not Rome's civilization, but rather an enemy within the gates) were it not that the values revealed by its behaviour have a disquieting affinity with some that we find among the patricians and that it is precisely their submission to its demands that calls forth the opposition from Coriolanus that prompted our inquiry. For the truth is that Shakespeare has sometimes drawn the patrician world in harsh, blunt lines. Bold, vigorous, and spirited, the Roman nobles are insensitive to nobility except for the specialized virtues of warfare and are redeemed largely by their generous respect for these qualities in each other and by the aristocratic imperturbability, the sarcastic detachment with which they face annihilation at the end.[1] Cominius is a

[1] Ironically, Coriolanus never sees the best of those aristocrats whom he hates for the sake of the city, the scenes in which, awaiting destruction in Rome, they mock the craven repentance of the 'clusters'. (IV. vi and V. i.)

good general, brave in war but no fire-eater, sensible and conciliatory in politics, knowing well the importance of Coriolanus's achievements and making a sane plea for public acknowledgment of it;[1] a just man but no idealist; a man who lets himself be guided by custom and events instead of shaping them. He, Menenius and Volumnia alike believe in maintaining a balance between ideals and complaisance; convictions are one thing; to act upon them implacably, as would Coriolanus, is another. Volumnia betrays this as often as she speaks of the Volscian wars,[2] but she adds much also that the other patricians do not openly express. There is something crude and coarse-grained in her enumeration of Coriolanus's wounds; at least half her pleasure is in their market-value, they are something 'to show to the people'.[3] Her restless ambition is short-sighted and limited, carrying in it the seeds of bitterness and ultimate defeat; her son has 'outdone his former deeds doubly',[4] but we question to what positive good this cumulative record-breaking is to lead. And so when she meets in him a resistance she cannot understand she assumes it to be a trivial folly.[5] But the reader, guided imperceptibly by signs invisible to her, begins to recognize that her limited and crude ambitions owe such dominion as they have over Coriolanus to childhood's training; his affections have made them in some sort sacred to him, the only images in which he could clothe his innate aspirations and ideals.

The ideals of this Rome in fact are sometimes base, and precisely because of their limitations;[6] Volumnia gloats over Coriolanus's wounds as a profitable investment, and crude butchery wins the respect even of Cominius, taking high place in his official speech to the Senate on Coriolanus's triumph.[7] If these are indeed the roots of Rome's code and values we have much ground for disquiet; perhaps, at the end of the play, as

[1] I. vi. I. ix, esp. 53–5.   [2] I. iii. II. i.   [3] II. i. 165–72.
[4] II. i. 151–2.   [5] III. ii.   [6] II. i. 216–20.
[7] II. ii. 87–127.

Coriolanus

we listen to Volumnia's noble prayer to Coriolanus for the Rome that has ruined him,[1] we hear also a discordant echo of her exultation over the slaughter in Corioli.[2] Perhaps, after all, the mob are but the crudest element in a state in which even the patricians sometimes accept low values and condone base customs. Cominius and Menenius admit fairly and frankly[3] that they deserve destruction for abandoning Coriolanus to the mob's decree and this is the belated recognition, by two of Rome's best men, that they have hitherto identified themselves with some of the very things he had denounced.

This, then, is the obverse of that image of Rome to whose service Coriolanus had once dedicated himself, and after the overturning of his world, it, or something very like it, takes the place of that earlier image in his mind. In Corioli he sees no other. As to those Roman friends with whom he had been in close and happy relationship – 'He could not stay to picke them in a pile Of noysome, musty Chaffe'. 'Rome and her rats' are no longer now 'at point of battle', but infamous allies.

But has this reversal come, after all, without all warning? Of the process by which Coriolanus finds his way from the first image of Rome to its opposite we can only guess, for it is hidden in silence – the silence of his disappearance into exile from a stage he had hardly quitted before, the silence of his strange new taciturnity and later the even deeper silence, though more significant, of smooth concealing speech.[4] But the new picture is so sharply defined that it seems to spring all but complete from some area of the mind where it has long been secretly forming. Can this be so? If this is Shakespeare's intention here, perhaps we shall find Coriolanus already, before the crisis of his fortunes, more nearly aware than he dare admit of the two Romes in his own mind; perhaps we, the readers, have had intimations offered us of that uneasy relationship.

Such intimations of the hidden depths of the mind we shall

---

[1] V. iii.   [2] II. i. 175–8.

[3] IV. vi. 112–18, 137–9. V. iv. 35–8.   [4] See below, p. 70.

seek most naturally at the points of fissure, those moments when his behaviour is most nearly inexplicable to us, to his fellows, and to himself. We go back to the passages, that is, when his recoil from the customs of his world is most evident; in his abnormal hatred of its praises and in his deep-seated loathing of the election tactics of the patricians. In the second, he only hates more deeply (though from widely differing motives) a tradition that the patricians themselves dislike; he and they are at one so far. But in the first, in his discourteous rebuff to courtesy, his wanton repudiation of popularity, that draws down Cominius's merited rebuke,[1] he finds unbearable something that the patricians approve, a ritual that for them has significance and value. This is a wide breach not to be explained away by modesty or even by vanity. 'It does offend my heart'.[2] We have no reason now to take these words at anything but their face value; something contaminates the acclamations and praises poured upon him, so that they touch him at heart; there is nausea in the recoil. And thereupon, we observe, he turns to the figure that has stood mute in the midst of the clamour, to Virgilia. 'My gracious silence, hayle.'[3] Perhaps these words too mean precisely what they say; perhaps there is there something lacking else in his world, a source of grace and wisdom, a silence the vehement cannot touch.

Light can be thrown back upon the question at this point by certain habits of speech that grow upon him towards the end of the play. The first clear signs of change appear when he parts from Cominius, Menenius, Volumnia, and Virgilia at the gates of Rome,[4] when both bearing and language begin to reflect the deep shock given to his spirit by his banishment. Already he is the 'lonely Dragon that his Fenne Makes fear'd, and talk'd of more than seene'.[5] Moreover, it is he now who counsels calm and submission, quoting what were formerly Volumnia's own stoic *sententiae*. He sets up certain barriers

[1] I. ix. 41–53.   [2] II. i. 185.   [3] II. i. 192.
[4] IV. i.   [5] IV. i. 29–31.

between them and himself by this ominous steadiness of demeanour, this unnatural, even and measured phrasing. He be-
haves like a man who has summoned up a stoic dignity to
compensate for loss, conceal a wound or deny humiliation; a
man who has lost at once his world and his integrity. From this
scene onward, the familiar outbursts of rage disappear.[1] Paradoxically, the shock appears to have integrated his character.
(More probably, as we already divine, it has cut deeply into it
and left him to rescue and integrate one part only.) From now,
he practises a rigid and seemingly unbreakable control over his
emotions, a cynical shrewdness in planning his treatment of
men, an unscrupulous exercise of flattery in subduing them.[2]
But, there are indications that this inflexible rigidity belongs
only to the surface of his mind and that is now the surface only
of a part. This demeanour is more ominous than the former,
ungoverned outbursts of rage or irritation; the man is for the
time hardly sane, though his madness does not touch, what
nothing has ever troubled, his military genius. He appears rather
as a man playing a part or a succession of parts and watching
himself as he does so.[3] And in the end this declares itself in a
habit of speech which throws light back over the whole play.

For again and again, especially in the crucial scene of the last
act, Coriolanus speaks of himself as an actor or as a man determined to deny nature.[4] The two recur in sinister conjunction

[1] To reappear once more only, at the end of the play, after his reconver-
sion.

[2] V. vi. 21–6, 71–84.

[3] This is an almost complete reversal of his former behaviour. The
modesty is gone and he courts publicity; resolved to 'exceed the common',
he deliberately makes himself 'feared and talked of'. His 'love's upon this
enemy town' and the measure of his reasoning delusion is to be found in
his assumption that he will not find in Antium the human nature he had
'banished' in Rome. He is as short-sighted in his estimate of Volscian hero-
worship as he was shrewd in his condemnation of the Roman.

[4] V. iii. 24–5, 35–7, 40–2, 83–4, 184–5.

and these related and iterative images begin to stir the reader's imagination.

The climax of this headlong career of perversity comes in the fifth act, when the man who revolted against a conventional untruth and hated even the semblance of exaggerated praise has now put his imagination at the service of deliberate fantasy and built between himself and the world a gigantic façade of megalomaniac shams. The familiar images of the actor recur here and the language and rhythms of his speech are a clear index of the severance of his conduct from his nature.[1] The complex syntax, the florid vocabulary, the imagery at once banal and theatrical, the slow and weighty rhythms that reverberate like a hollow structure are as far removed from those of the earlier acts, from the ringing athletic movement, the crisp hammer-blows of the syntax and the vivid, shining imagery, as this later Coriolanus is from the gallant and impetuous aristocrat of the beginning.

We ask ourselves whether this seemingly new habit is of purely recent growth, derived solely from his spirit's catastrophe and sequent experience, or whether this, like that major image, the new picture of the Roman state, has its roots also in some earlier phase, had already, in fact, been long preparing in secret recesses of his mind. And this question leads us back again to the middle of the play, to the triumphant return from the Volscian war and to the consular elections. For it is upon these scenes that we must turn such light as we can derive from the final phases of Coriolanus's behaviour.

'It is a part that I shall blush in acting.'[2] The words are spoken in protest to his fellow patricians when they urge him to put on the 'vesture of humility' and beg the people's votes in the open forum. And in a later scene he recurs at intervals to this image.[3] To his fellow-patricians, this is something to be

---

[1] Especially in V. iii. 56–67, and 183–9. On the rhythms of Coriolanus's speech here see also *post* p. 135.

[2] II. ii. 149–50.

[3] III. ii. 15–16, 105–6 (109–10, Volumnia), 112–15.

Coriolanus

argued away by appeals to common sense and to custom, even if need be, by Volumnia's impatient scolding. But the disproportionate outbursts of anger as he resists and the persistent returns to the image that accompany them point to something genuine in the words and deeper in the motive. Nor is the cause of it the pride of which Volumnia and the tribunes accuse him.[1] It is clear that he fears some consequences far graver than they, who think only of the practical effects, and that though his fear is instinctive and only half-articulate, he is aware of some deep inward harm that threatens if he consents. And as the pressure upon him increases, in the later scene (III. ii), and his resistance becomes more desperate, we realize that he is right, though he cannot communicate his reasons to them. Their demand is dastardly and his ultimate consent disastrous, not because his failure brings ruin on him, but because the result is precisely what he foretells, and because in consenting to play a part he does indeed 'teach his Minde a most inherent Baseness'.[2] To them the impersonation that they counsel is a sensible piece of complaisance and no man of the world would think twice of it. But to him the pretence, the attempt to be something other than himself, means the forfeit of his integrity. What follows, from the decision of III. iii to the end of the play is determined by this and if Coriolanus, after the shock of his banishment, appears to hide himself in a succession of parts, culminating in that of the inhuman world-conqueror which Volumnia herself is compelled to destroy, it is because he has lost the power to 'honor mine owne truth',[3] and has no other

---

[1] The word 'pride' is used nearly a dozen times in the course of the play and some six or seven of the other characters agree in thus accusing him; the first citizen, Sicinius (twice), the first Senate Officer, Brutus (twice), Volumnia (III. ii. 126, 130 and V. iii. 170) and Aufidius, explicitly in IV. vii. 8 and by implication from that point onward. But it is to be noticed that all but one of these are prejudiced utterances; even Volumnia's are to clinch an argument or reinforce an appeal.

[2] III. ii. 120–3.   [3] III. ii. 121.

stay against the tide of hitherto unknown passions that sweep him onward.

If, moreover, we were right in thinking that this baser Rome, present alike in the easy-going patricians and in the violent and sentimental mob, acted unconsciously as an irritant in Coriolanus's mind, if we are persuaded that, by conceding to it the service of a lie, he has in his own eyes forfeited his honour and debased his mind, if we think that his loss of the integrity that had upheld him is the real cause of the histrionic and vindictive treachery of the last acts, can we go a step further and ask why this experience, which Volumnia would have carried so lightly, brings psychological disaster to her son? If we would do this, we must attempt to guess at what has all this while lain hidden, that part of Coriolanus's nature which was not expressed in the double career of heroic soldier and forthright but discerning statesman, that part which was outraged by the customs his closest friends took as matters of course, that part whose resistance was broken by his own consent to a lie. I think that here too Shakespeare has given us certain impressions that can guide us to a conclusion justified in the context of the play.

Some words of Volumnia's spoken at the height of her exasperation when Coriolanus, after winning their votes, has provoked the mob to fury, surprise us by their evident misunderstanding of the nature of his impulse. 'You might have beene enough the man you are With striuing lesse to be so.'[1] Is there any truth in this or is it in fact valuable precisely as a mis-reading of his character serving to point us to an opposite truth? For, despite his confusion, Coriolanus appears to be striving rather to be the man he is, a man, it may be, that neither he nor she knows; the very fact of the strife is perhaps an index of his frustration. She accuses him of being 'too absolute'[2] and, again, this absoluteness may but indicate a man not yet on terms with himself and struggling to preserve what

[1] III. ii. 19–20.   [2] III. ii. 39.

he cannot define. Her argument here [1] that the union of 'honour and policy' in war are a true parallel to the conduct she now urges upon him is specious and fallacious. For uprightness and deliberate deception in a statesman are incompatible, while valour and strategy in war are not. 'They do not go together', [2] and this he certainly knows even if he cannot define or articulate his knowledge. The strife that is native to his mind is not this deep, inward conflict, but a forthright, eager strife for some glory, that cannot be measured or satisfied by success. It is a great part of his tragedy that this glory is undefined; nevertheless, his desire for it fires his valour as does Tamburlaine's aspiration or Hotspur's 'bright honour'. It has no commerce with Volumnia's well-defined aims of power and dominion. [3] The Coriolanus we see in the play, for lack of a clearer sight or worthier image, struggles to satisfy this passion for glory with things that breed in him disquiet and disgust. The state he serves, the class to which his love and loyalty are bound, are content with mundane aims baser than his, with ideals that offer him no scope. [4] The preoccupation with his rival Aufidius, [5] which appears early in the play, may be but another indication of this restless search for an ideal objective; Aufidius becomes in some sort a focus, though but a nebulous one, for this desire for splendour of life that the summit of achievement in Rome could never offer. Antium, 'this Enemie Towne', [6] already in the third act calls forth a line ironic but also prophetic, 'I wish I had a cause to seeke him there'. [7] In this passionate desire to image an undefined aspiration (and, it may be, unrecognized ideals) Antium becomes the city of his dreams. 'A goodly City

[1] III. ii. 47–57, 58–61, 62–4. [2] (*A.C.* IV. xv. 47.) [3] II. i. 188–94.

[4] Volumnia to the end never perceives this, but two other characters, Cominius and Menenius, come near to doing so when in the fourth and fifth acts they acknowledge that his fellow patricians have in some sort betrayed Coriolanus and identified themselves with what was base and contemptible in Rome.

[5] I. i. 236–8. [6] IV. iv. 23–4. [7] III. i. 19.

is this *Antium*,[1] and the violent recoil from Rome in the fourth act makes it certain that he will rush to embrace that world that his imagination has already sought in secret. For what has all along looked like pride in Coriolanus is but rebellion against standards and concessions that repel him; the reaction has been negative, disgust and repudiation, because he cannot focus his aspiration, but aspiration is there in him, as strong as ever it was in Hotspur or Tamburlaine, though stifled and perverted.

And so we return to the words whose significance we hoped to illuminate with the help of secret impressions made upon us by other passages in the play. 'My gracious silence, hayle!' The words are sometimes read as a kindly, half-teasing greeting; affectionate and gently bantering. If we have come near the truth in what we have suggested already, they will now mean more than this. They may well be the only overt expression in the play of two things deeply hidden in the mind of Coriolanus, of a longing for the balancing silences, graces, and wisdom banished from the outer world but vital to wholeness of life, and an acknowledgement, albeit inarticulate, that in Virgilia these values were preserved. The clamour around him is his everyday condition, the easily articulated code of his community, at once heroic and insidiously base, the only system of values he has seen defined. But the source of aspiration such as his, an instinctive longing for poetry of living,[2] con-

[1] IV. iv. 1, cf. III. iii. 133.
[2] Certain of Coriolanus's images bear out this. It is at first glance surprising that he does not, like Antony, draw his images from the battle-field, but sometimes, both in the earlier and in the later part of the play, from a quite different world of fancy or imagination. There are sudden, momentary flights from the immediate and actual; in the midst of his abuse of the mob comes the picture of them throwing up their caps, not as though they would lodge them on the Capitol, but 'as they would hang them on the hornes o' th' Moone' (I. i. 217) and from the often hollow imagery of Act V, scene iii, there flashes out the description of Valeria 'Chaste as the Icicle

Coriolanus

tains within it an innate love for silence and grace and even for that Valley of Humiliation whose air Bunyan knew to be sweeter than all others. His need is for wholeness of life and he has harnessed the poetry of living to battle and bloodshed. What his aspiration sought of life was that it should be radiant, clear and significant. And for this bread of life his world has offered him success and dominion preserved at the price of complaisance.

> I thinke hee'l be to Rome
> As is the Aspray to the Fish, who takes it
> By Soueraignty of Nature.[1]

This sovereignty, this greatness is probably our final impression, that and the simplicity inseparable from greatness that has been his undoing. It is not the military greatness that his fellow-soldiers Roman and Volscian acclaim throughout the play, though that is a partial image of it. It is something that they cannot define, in spite of their many attempts at definition,[2] yet it is something that each in turn perceives, gladly or grudgingly, and the reiteration of the word noble [3] reveals their

---

That's curdied by the Frost from purest Snow, And hangs on Dians Temple' (V. iii. 65–6). Images from nature thus break through, 'pebbles' and stars, the 'mutinous windes' that 'Strike the proud Cedars 'gainst the fiery Sun' (V. iii. 60) and are at once in sharp contrast with the hyperbole and self-consciousness of the actor and suggestive of something escaping from the depths of his mind under the final strain of this scene. My attention was first drawn to the presence of these images in Coriolanus's speech by Miss Jacqueline R. Dunn.

[1] IV. vii. 35.

[2] I. iv. 52–61; III. i. 254–9; (IV. v. 66–8); IV. vii. 33–5, 48–53; (V. vi. 126–8).

[3] Some twenty-five in all are spoken of Coriolanus, but the word has echoes in the traditional application to the patricians as description of rank

Shakespeare the Dramatist

momentary recognitions. But an unholy alliance between the debased and limited ideals of his world and the heart's affections that a meaner man would have put aside has impressed upon his imagination an image of that ideal as insufficient for him as it was too great for the thing it imaged. This magnitude of spirit and imagination was moulded from birth in the worship of the Roman state. But in time that imagination substituted for itself an ideal Rome, as, later, an ideal Antium, both nobler than the actual and indeed non-existent. This was the inevitable result of the attempt to bind such potentialities within such limitations and its outcome could only be the destruction of one or both. The movement towards destruction set in when, under pressure of the Roman state and its ideals, Coriolanus renounced his own undefined but hitherto unquenched aspiration. Then the surest principle of his being was contaminated and the sovereignty of his nature perverted.

I have attempted to show here, as in other parts of this book, that it is by secret impressions that Shakespeare conveys to our imaginations the nature of such a character as Coriolanus. So great is the contradiction between his outward seeming and his hidden self, so blinded and incomplete his self-knowledge, that nothing but some such disclosure could have led us to understanding (imperfect though it is) and nothing but the supreme tact of an evocative mode could have pointed us the way. Coriolanus cannot himself reveal to us his nature and motives, for part of that nature is denied and part undeveloped. No other character in the play can direct us, for the presence of such a person, articulate and clear-sighted, would have provided him with an ally against his own confusion and the limitations of

and the somewhat similar use among the Volscian gentry. The following are some of the references to Coriolanus: I. i. 169, 253; I. iv. 52; I, ix. 66; II. ii. 45, 134; II. iii. 9, 93, 141; III. i. 233, 254; III. ii. 40; IV. ii. 21; IV. v. 68, 112, 122 (all spoken by Aufidius); IV. vi. 109; IV. vii. 36; V. iii. 145, 154; V. vi. 126, 145, 155. (Aufidius's earlier images and 'devil', 'viper', etc.)

his world. Only Virgilia seems to preserve for him some source of peace, silence, and wonder from which the thirst of his spirit can be assuaged and it is in his words to her that we find one of the most potent of those secret impressions that work powerfully upon the imagination.

V

The Nature of Plot in Drama

IF WE APPROACH THE play by way of plot instead of by way of character, we shall reach similar conclusions. For since character, plot, imagery, language, verbal music are only aspects of the indivisible whole which is the play, whatever we discover in one of them to be essential to the whole will reveal itself also in others. We separate them by virtue of an agreed convention. But in relation to the whole and to each other they are inseparable; each may in fact appear at times to be an aspect of another, since their territories are ultimately indivisible. And just as what drama presents to our imagination as character differs from what life presents, so is it with plot, which is not identical with a series of actual events or even with the groups of events that sometimes seem to emerge in life. Each has a similar relation to its counterpart in what we call the actual world in that in each the artist's imagination has selected from the raw material on which his inspiration worked and revealed a pattern inherent in it. And the nature of this imaginative selection is determined by the mode of the dramatist, so that in every aspect of the technique we may trace a corresponding pattern in harmony with the form of the whole to which it contributes.[1] Each aspect of the technique, then, plays its part in revealing the dramatist's apprehension of life, but plot may fitly follow character here since they merge naturally into each other through the continuous interplay between individual character and even within a given play.

[1] On the nature of the patterns defined by selection something has already been said in Chapter III.

78

The Nature of Plot in Drama

Plot, indeed, whether simple or complex, single or multiple, may be said to have two aspects, the spatial, which is concerned with character-grouping, and the temporal, which has regard to the order and relation of events.[1] The first, like a picture or a statuary group, may be thought of (if we adopt Lessing's distinction)[2] as static in time and extended in space and in studying it we consider the characters not in terms of their experience or of their effect upon the plot, but in terms of the illumination we receive from their juxtaposition and their relative positions in the composition. The other approach to plot shows it as extended in time and gives us the ordered sequence of causally related events. This again appears, upon closer inspection, to have two strands, the inner and the outer plot or drama, both moving continuously forward in time, both intermittently revealed and inseparably related.[3] The differences in mode that we have already observed may be traced in both these aspects of the plot and in both levels of the second.

Thus, in the spatial aspect a dramatist of one kind will use a design which itself seems to demonstrate some theme or argument, a logical, expository grouping that constitutes an explanation or furnishes a key to some problem, reminding us sometimes of the Victorian narrative school of painting in which the picture 'told a story'. Another, having no demonstrable theme, problem, or thesis, having no palpable design upon his drama and no purpose but the artist's fundamental

---

[1] The intimacy of the relationship between character and plot again becomes clear when we consider that the grouping of character may be regarded either as the structural aspect of character or the spatial aspect of plot. Upon the spatial aspect of plot, see G. Wilson Knight, *The Wheel of Fire*, Chap. I.

[2] See *Laokoon*. Chaps. XV–XVIII. 'Es bleibt dabei: die Zeitfolge ist das Gebiet des Dichters, so wie der Raum das Gebiet des Malers.' (Chap. XVIII.)

[3] The relations of these two levels of plot within the time continuum admit obviously of wide variety in kind and spacing.

79

purpose of making a work of art, will reveal wholly different implications through the composition of his picture.

The first will present a carefully planned range of characters that balance each other as in Ibsen's *Ghosts*,[1] where the five are so selected that each contributes to the central idea of the play one part of the final, composite effect. The dead hand of convention and obligation has subdued to its purposes Pastor Manders, who has thus become its vehicle and its exponent, but it has driven Mrs Alving to rebellion and so to emancipa-- tion of thought. Modifying the contrasted positions of these two are three others who show the workings of the compulsion upon related, yet differing, types of mind and character. Each is a variation on the central theme and the whole group indicates the salient effects, and in representative proportions: Regine has rebelled without thought or heart-searching and has suffered the degeneration that comes of rejecting the good and the bad alike in a given social code; her 'father', Engstrand, as immoral as she but more shrewd, has cunningly observed the workings of the system and found his account in playing upon its victims; Osvald has escaped psychological harm only to be destroyed by the physical consequences from which nothing could save him. Each bears mute or articulate testimony to the weight of this dead hand and their relationship demonstrates the operation of the curse; a Laocoon group, figures still imprisoned or too late emancipated to maintain valid life.

But another dramatist may relate his characters in such a way that, instead of a close-locked group, itself the image of the operation of a force, with each member sustaining an essential part of the whole in strict relation of contrast and likeness to the others, we find characters widely differing as individuals or as groups, and so placed that our imaginations are induced to supply, it may be at unawares, intermediate and background figures or moods that complete a harmony of wide range and

[1] See below, p. 143.

complexity, suggesting to our minds not a clear-cut image or a dominant theme, but the breadth of life and of humanity. We recognize that without such subtlety of relationship between the figures in the picture there would be no harmony, but only a scattering of portraits, vivid it might be and even varied, but giving no significance to the content of the play. Somewhere in the dramatist's way of relating them lies the stimulus to which our imaginations respond; here we may find secret impressions conveyed by the grouping itself. Shakespeare in as early a play as *A Midsummer Night's Dream* already prompts us by the spatial aspect of his plot alone to the 'generation of still breeding thoughts' by which we 'people this little world'.

And what a range this world has! Our first glance shows us princes and their subjects, townsfolk, peasants, and craftsmen; lovers, parents, and children; the wide variety of personality which ranges from the judicial magnanimity of Theseus to the crabbed Egeus, the unmoral fairy world, the childish egotism of the young lovers and the hearty freedom of the peasants. But delicate threads of relationship join these figures or groups into a more complex and subtle pattern. Theseus and Hippolyta are princes, but so also are Oberon and Titania; even Bottom is the born ruler of his village community. Hermia, Helena, Lysander, and Demetrius are lovers after one fashion, but so, after another and a better, are Theseus and Hippolyta, and so in their strange way are Oberon and Titania. Not only are there the human relations of parent and child, lover and lover, but also a wide range of age, from the old Egeus and the mature Theseus to the four young lovers, all made significant by the constant presence of the ageless, immortal fairies. At the centre still is Theseus, the responsible father of his people, at once submitting to and upholding the social order of his dukedom; but the individualists Bottom and Puck are there too, each absorbed, in delighted preoccupation, with fantasies humdrum or exquisite of his own creating. And so the network spreads, linking, each to each, characters in all else disparate and seemingly unrelated. Each figure in a play whose spatial structure is of this kind is like an illuminated point, independent and set at a distance from each of the others; yet seemingly endless patterns now suggest themselves by linking each to several others and the central figure to all. There is here no palpable intention of suggesting by the disposal of the characters the multitudinous complexity of life, still less of laying upon each the task of sustaining its share of an emergent idea. But the imaginary line that flashes from one corner to another of the picture passes through (and gathers up by its passing) many who are not present in the play. Prince, townsman, peasant, craftsman, reveal when we link them the invisible presence of intermediate 'occupations' and 'trades'. And the fairies, creatures of yet another kind, set off and illuminate by contrast the human groups and their organisation. Age, maturity, youth suggest between them the span of human life, but the ageless fairies reveal by their timelessness the significance of time which determines human life. And what our imaginations receive is an impression not of a theme or of an idea but of a world and a life in which every individual is essentially itself and not primarily a part of a thematic design, but in which, nevertheless, each is related to others by contrast or likeness of age, sex, function, or temperament, so that none can be thought of for long in isolation. But it is the secret impressions that have given us the sense of this; the imaginary lines which linked light to light and drew out from their background of invisibility those hidden figures whose momentary and imagined presence made up the world in which the people of the play lived and were at home. The function of the dramatic mode here is to enrich, fill out, and if need be modify the image of the world that surrounds and reveals itself through the characters.[1] Just so, when we con-

[1] The nature of this kind of spatial structure becomes clearer still if we set beside it yet another play of Ibsen, *The Pillars of the Community*, whose character grouping might appear at first glance to resemble that of *A*

The Nature of Plot in Drama

sidered these as individuals, it was seen to reveal the fuller world within each character.

At an earlier period of dramatic history the genius of Aeschylus evokes in like way an image of a play's world by the placing of its characters. Agamemnon is a prince, like Clytemnestra; an Argive, as are the chorus and all the other characters except Cassandra; he is linked with Clytemnestra by marriage and parenthood; with Aegisthus by blood relationship and the common heritage of the Thyestean curse; with the soldier who announces his homecoming by the ties of profession and the long experience of the siege of Troy; with the sentinel, who is his faithful servant, by Argos; and with Cassandra again by the common background of the Trojan war and of princely birth. Clytemnestra, too, has other links not only with him, but with Aegisthus as her lover, as a home-dwelling Argive and finally as fellow-murderer. Cassandra alone stands in an isolation which links her by very contrast; no longer a prince but a captive, the only Trojan among the home-keeping Argives and the returning Argive army, young in a world of the mature and the old, cut off even by her foreign speech, yet

---

Midsummer Night's Dream. The relations between the many strands of action and the direct links between the numerous characters reveal to a careful inspection the fact that the most seemingly detached of these strands are related to at least three or four others. But there is a palpable purpose behind this only less evident than that behind the statuesque grouping of the characters in *Ghosts.* Again, the characters are related to certain problems and responsible for revealing them. They are so placed not so much to imply a world of men as to contribute to a balance of forces. Through them all runs the dominant theme of Bernick's conversion, the progress of his soul through crime and punishment to redemption. Ibsen gathers up and puts into Bernick's hands all the threads of the plot and consequently all the responsibility. We assist throughout the play at an inevitable progress to a triumphant demonstration. But the function of the spatial aspect is to contribute to our understanding of the emergent theme, rather than to extend the implications of the play.

Shakespeare the Dramatist

driven by Apollo to join her fate with Agamemnon's. By these six characters and the lines that link them we are made aware of three worlds: the Argive polity, its inheritance, and its doom; the fallen greatness of the Trojan civilization; and the darkly triumphant Argive army that has lain ten years encamped before Troy. Each of the characters sustains a share, not in the disclosure of a theme (that task is laid upon the chorus), but in revealing and suggesting the fates and history of one or other of these three worlds of men. And thus our impression of the immense scope of the play derives simultaneously from the choric comments and from awareness of wider worlds evoked by the lines that link the characters by contrast and likeness.[1] This is true also of the other plays of Aeschylus, of Sophocles, and of Euripides. Even in the more primitive *Supplices*, where the clash of two civilizations is the evident substance of the play, the links, though less subtle, bear still an essential part of extending the scope. In the *Bacchae* of Euripides at the other end of the period, we discern the same net-work of lines with the same functions as in the late work of Aeschylus, but approaching now nearer to the multitudinous evocation of Shakespeare's structure. And so we find the evocative technique of the essential dramatist at work in the spatial structure of his plays, while it is deliberately replaced by another mode in the corresponding structure of a philosophical dramatist such as Ibsen. In the Greek drama and that derived from the Greek as is Racine's, the characters are few and, except for an occasional subsidiary figure, are spread across the foreground; the design imposed on the production by the shallow Greek

---

[1] The same function of spatial relations may be traced in the work of that later poet who is, by discipline and devotion, chief heir to the Greek dramatic genius. In some seven at least of the plays of Racine the few characters extend the scope of the drama by drawing into the spatial plot a wide range of worlds or associations. This is perhaps most clearly seen in *Andromaque* and *Bérénice*, but it is at work also in *Mithridate*, *Iphigénie*, *Phèdre*, *Esther*, and *Athalie*.

stage thus finds its analogue in the positions of the characters in the spatial design of the play.

But in the plays of Shakespeare's maturity, we perceive a third dimension, akin to the depth given by perspective to a painting; in dimensions and tone alike the characters retreat successively from the foreground towards a background where they reach a virtual vanishing point.[1] In the play of *Antony and*

[1] This technique in painting is, of course, common and elementary knowledge. But even at the risk of offering a naïve comment, I should like to describe those aspects which appear relevant also to the study of drama. This footnote should obviously be passed over by those who know the elements of the technique of painting and, even more obviously, by those who paint.

The familiar ways of conveying the impression of distance are by the perspective of line and of colour; in line by diminution of size in identical objects and in colour by diminution of tone or change of line. Thus, both in nature and in painting, we observe fewer distinctive characteristics as objects become more distant and, as a corollary, they make less claim on the attention. This does not imply that they appear less real. A tree at a distance does not normally appear unreal; it is merely, by reason of its position, less individualized than a tree in the foreground. We can see the pattern of the window-curtain in the house across the road; we cannot distinguish even the windows in a farm near Calais seen from Dover Beach. But we accept both as houses. Moreover, in both the trees and the houses, loss of size has been accompanied by loss of tone (or brilliance of hue). When the atmosphere does not contribute a colour of its own, grey, blue, purple, increasing in proportion to the distance, we are able to observe pure loss of tone with distance. This can conveniently be done in, for instance, the Painted Desert of Arizona, where objects eighty miles away will be found surprisingly to retain some of their colour, but to retain it in diluted form. This may perhaps be regarded as a case of pure colour perspective, since nothing has been added by 'veils' of atmosphere. Even when atmosphere does interfere, there is still a true relationship between line and colour perspective, though it may sometimes take a fantastic form; when one is painting a tree in a London fog, the furthest branch may be reduced to a pale grey, while the nearest is dark and vivid and hardly any linear perspective is noticed. The law is ultimately the same: with increasing

Shakespeare the Dramatist

Cleopatra the magnitude of the issues, the grandeur of the chief characters, the multiplicity of figures and events witness to the vastness of its design and the cosmic imagery leads the imagination on to a universe beyond, into which the immediate world of the play seems limitlessly extended. The spatial structure too plays its own, considerable part in this final impression. The spatial relations of the characters may be traced as they were in *A Midsummer Night's Dream* and the amplitude of the later play is then seen to embrace the whole known world. But just as in a painting the sense of vastness may be given not only by the spread of the foreground, but also by depth and distance,[1] so, in

---

distance there must be both reduction of size and dilution of colour; though the one may have its maximum effect and the other its minimum, in any given scene there must be a consistent relationship between the two. What is essential is the diminishing potency of the object in the picture. The loss of tone also accounts for the loss of detail; the main patches of colour are themselves diluted, the shadows grow paler, the highlights dimmer until there is, at a sufficient distance, no distinction between the three. Anyone who attempts to paint mountain or desert scenery recognizes this regressive loss of tone, its contribution to the sense of distance and the relative inability of linear perspective to achieve this by itself.

Just as certain painters (Cuyp, Van Goyen, Capelle, Hendrik Avercamp) achieve the effect of great distance and depth of scene by continuous and simultaneous perspective of line and colour, so, too, certain dramatists use a corresponding technique in the spatial structure of their plays.

Nor, as we have said, does this recession from the foreground of the play rob the characters or episodes of reality, but only of distinction in detail. The essential reality of the minor figures remains up to the verge of visibility (at which point a sentry's only speech may be 'My Lord?'). Here, admittedly, it is hard to find individuality and it would be an ill-constructed drama in which we could, for a dramatist, though aware of the reality of even the least of his minors, will nevertheless reduce him to an almost invisible figure if his function in the play sets him in the far distant background.

[1] Frith's *Ramsgate Sands* is a long, crowded ribbon of figures that gives little sense of distance, but Hendrik Avercamp's *Winter* (a far smaller canvas) is a wide and melancholy plain of ice, its distances defined by diminishing

a play, the relative proportions in function and the relative vividness in personality complete that impression of extent already made upon us by greatness of scope, character, and event. In the greatest plays, moreover, distance itself gives prominence to the chief characters; the attention of the subordinate agents is focused upon them, investing them with significance which draws some of its potency from their spatial relations. A whole universe, it seems, is intent upon the action of those foreground figures and their power in turn reaches to the uttermost bounds of the world, to figures upon the very border of invisibility. The dramatic function of perspective in *Antony and Cleopatra* is to evoke, by this secret impression, the sense at once of vastness, of coherence, and of significance.

When we attempt to group in the mind's eye the figures in this play, we are struck at once by the operation of a simple law; those that are most vivid in personality are also those that have the most important functions. A character of relatively minor importance who makes a brief appearance in an early scene and with no evident or immediate promise of a greater part to play later, yet stirs the imagination and remains vividly in our minds, will almost invariably appear again in a later scene when his function will be graver or weightier. The marks of such a character may be of various kinds; the language he speaks, his imagery, or a noticeable habit of syntax; the attention he draws to himself from other characters; a peculiar relation to one of the main characters, even if it is only our own emotional response to him; some light thrown upon him by the attitude of that other or by some comment drawn from him. This, which we may describe as the colour or tone initially given to a minor character, will be found to correspond, when the whole play is before us, with the function assigned

---

figures, progressively smaller and fainter. The element of continuous regression, found in many Dutch landscapes with figures, is of vital importance to the impression of depth and distance.

him, with his ultimate position in the plot. Characters, on the other hand, whose initial speeches seem curiously colourless in view of the number of scenes in which they promise to appear, turn out to have in fact little function beyond that of frequently standing on the stage; they do not speak much or contribute much; they are found to be as limited in their ultimate function as they are in their initial colour. There is thus, it would appear, a consistent relation between what, reverting to our pictorial image, we may call colour and size and as scene succeeds scene in the temporal plot of the play it tends to reveal the same tonal relation between the characters in it as does the total spatial plot.

Setting aside then the main characters, whose prominence no one proposes to question, we may fairly expect to discover continuous regression in the spatial grouping of the minor figures. And it is upon continuity in regression that a great part of the depth of the play's focus depends. Behind the first ten or twelve figures, who themselves recede and diminish in size and colour from Antony and Cleopatra to Maecenas, Agrippa, and Alexas, come those of further diminishing proportions, Scarus, Dolabella, Menecrates, Mardian, Canidius, with behind them again, Ventidius, Thyreus, the clown, the Soothsayer, Dercetas, Diomed. In all these, function and colour, though growing ever slighter and fainter, are still distinct, while behind them range a number of figures, growing steadily less distinct, servants, messengers, soldiers, guards, some thirty-five or -six of them, the ultimate horizon being represented by the virtually invisible Taurus (of III. viii. 21) whose total contribution to the play is the line 'My Lord?'

Now it is somewhere within this range, from Scarus to Taurus, that the principle of continuous regression in character grouping will finally be revealed, for it is these minor figures who between them define the furthest depths of the scene. Scarus appears in three scenes,[1] though he only speaks in

[1] III. viii; IV. vii; IV. viii.

The Nature of Plot in Drama

the first two and has only ten speeches, some twenty-five lines, in all. But the five speeches in III. viii are full of rich and memorable imagery, part comic, part poetic, the vehement language and syntax of wrath and abuse. We recognize the clear colours of the character; an experienced officer involved in a defeat, a brave, high-hearted soldier. He stands out at once from the background of soldiers, guards and messengers who appear once and then disappear and in the second and third scenes his function grows to match the vividness with which his character was first drawn. He supports and encourages Antony helping to turn the tide of war, and is then drawn forward out of the background by the warmth and understanding of Antony's words to Cleopatra. The sharpness of colour which caught the eye in his first three or four short speeches was, then, a true index of his position and of a function ultimately greater than we should have expected.

Behind him again are more figures who belong to the ever receding background and mark its depth by their ever decreasing colour and magnitude. The soldier who bears the news of Enobarbus's desertion[1] has but five speeches so brief that they total only about seven lines; something of his character is allowed to appear, sturdy, loyal, uncompromising, even provocative. And this degree of individuality is warranted by his function; he is the means of revealing the gentleness of Antony on the eve of a great battle and calls forth the expression of the General's generous understanding of Enobarbus. The slight figure of this soldier is thus so placed and so coloured that it illuminates one side of Antony's character. Of corresponding dimensions and tone are the soldier who in III. vi bears Enobarbus's treasure to him from Antony, the messenger of I. iii and Silius in III. i. And close to them in the grouping, but diminished and paler, are the soldier of III. vii and Diomed in IV. xii and V. i.

At a little further distance we come upon figures such as

[1] IV. v.

Seleucus, the Messenger of I. ii, the two servants of II. vii, and the guard of V. ii. The few lines of Seleucus (he has only three, divided between three speeches) contain more colour than their brevity might suggest, but the function of the disloyal servant has a moment's sharp significance and so the colour of his speech, for the moment too matches it, slight though both are.

We are approaching the vanishing point now, where Taurus disappears with his two-word speech, but to the very edge of visibility the figures maintain their simultaneous diminution of function and tone. The four soldiers who in IV. iii listen to the mysterious music on the eve of Antony's defeat, being charged with the function of heightening, in their short scene, the effect of anticipation and of revealing the perilous psychological balance of Antony's troops, have yet just enough individual tone to be distinguishable from each other and the first, with his nine short speeches contained in seven lines, is the leader; he can hear the music and shows some initiative in investigating it. The second, more imaginative and apprehensive, hazards an interpretation. The anxiety of the third only echoes the other speakers point by point and the fourth shows a steady if imaginative optimism. The last three share between them fourteen speeches in about as many lines, but the faint indications of character can still be seen. Behind them and fainter yet are Varrius, the second and third soldiers of IV. ix, the three guards of IV. xii, the messenger of I. ii, Demetrius, the Egyptian of V. i, and the messenger of III. vii. The last two are as nearly colourless and functionless as it is possible to be while yet serving some purpose in the background of the play and are only slightly removed from the invisibility of the vanishing-point. But their function is nevertheless indispensable, for they define the last positions in that continuous regression which has given depth and distance to the spatial aspect of the play and completed the impression of its magnitude.

★

The Nature of Plot in Drama

If we look at the temporal aspects of that ordered sequence of events that we call the plot, we find that this also is affected by the mode of the dramatist; one will present a logically articulated series and the other reveal what the poet has divined by inducing a continuing or developing experience in the mind of reader or audience. The first is the counterpart of the self-explanatory characters and the demonstrative spatial plot that we have just described. The other is associated with the process that reveals or modifies character by half-hidden signs and plots by leaving our imaginations to supply (it may be all unawares) the events needed to complete the full graph by linking together crucial events or scenes.

The coherence given to the first kind of plot by the logic of event serves a philosopher dramatist to emphasize his underlying idea and is indeed almost inseparable from his mode of writing. It is found in its finest form in the middle work of Ibsen, where the architectural power of the master building governs the relation of events, the indication of cause and effect by a precise articulation of the details of the plot. Each episode, each piece of setting, each section of dialogue, by its content, by its timing and by its placing, contributes directly to a design whose purpose is to set before us an interlocking series of events such as shall leave us no conclusion but the one Ibsen intends us to draw. The opening passages of these plays often fulfil four or five functions simultaneously, all directly or indirectly connected with the elucidation and the disengaging of the theme. This flawless, economical integration of the parts with the whole and with each other gives its own impression of inevitability; the sequence of events constitutes a demonstration. This is the natural way for him to use structure to demonstrate his theme. A usual but not an inseparable consequence of this compact and coherent plotting is the brevity of its dramatic time. The ultimate causes of the events presented to us lie far back in the past and Ibsen must bring them before our eyes by some form of recollection or reminiscence, but the occasion or immediate cause of word, deed, or event within the play is followed closely by its consequence and the final stages of the demonstration are before us in detail. So full is this detail that it may mislead us into thinking that the dramatist has given us the fulness of life itself.[1]

This logical and coherent ordering of the sequence of events, though only used in the drama of high seriousness by the philosophical dramatist has been understood from relatively early times by dramatists with other purposes. Even if the dramatist has no theme for the demonstrative technique to define by the three means we have already described, he may yet take a purely artistic delight in its design. The relations of cause and effect within each subsidiary plot and more still the relation between them, take on, in the hands of some dramatists of superlative skill, the beauty that always belongs to subtly related rhythms and curves of movement, such as those of a corps de ballet or a flock of seagulls in spring. In such cases, the content of the play is usually comic; the finest comedy of intrigue is of this kind and Terence and Plautus mastered it long ago. Sometimes a mind of musical or it may be of mathematical bent will design a complex plot the intricate relations and variations of whose curves are themselves a delight to us and, we must presume, to him. Perhaps no dramatist has ever touched Ben Jonson in this special domain. He did not use it in his tragedies, but in the near-tragedy of *Volpone* and in the

---

[1] This specific artistic discipline was one that could be learnt by Ibsen's successors and its influence may be traced in the work of Galsworthy and Granville-Barker in England and of Brieux in France. Few clearer instances could be found than Galsworthy's *Strife*, a play in which the addition of symmetry in the two subsidiary plots which combine to form the whole plot gives an almost euclidian finality to the demonstration. Barker's *Voysey Inheritance*, though less economical and less compact, belongs to the same family. It continues to appear in varying degree in many of the dramatists concerned with social problems; *Hindle Wakes*, *Chains*, and *Jane Clegg* all appear to owe something to it.

The Nature of Plot in Drama

bitter satire of *The Alchemist* we find a comedy whose rhythms hold strange commerce with 'The laws that keep The planets in their radiant courses.' But there is no theme here to be served and the only 'precepts deep' we are like to meet at the hands of Ben Jonson's rascals are curiously congruous with those of Praed's worthy vicar. The strength, swiftness, and precision of Ben Jonson's draughtmanship carries the technique of this particular kind of plot to achievements it does not usually reach, except in the process of demonstrating a theme. But it must be admitted that in the humbler domain of farce many a play has been saved from worthlessness by the taut, athletic movements and the logic (it may be fantastic) of its plot; by a strict disposal of the relations of cause and effect the more noticeable perhaps in that this is the only kind of artistic virtue farce is free to practise.

Now Shakespeare's mode which reveals the character of Coriolanus and the magnitude of the spatial design in *Antony and Cleopatra* by secret impressions made upon our imaginations makes an utterly different disposal of the ordered sequence of events that constitute the temporal aspect of the plot. These are not now compact, nor, on the plane of actual event, closely coherent. There are wide gaps in the sequence, to be leapt by the imagination, and these spaces or intervals have not a merely negative but a positive function. This becomes clear when we consider what is in fact omitted in some of the greatest of his plays from the material he might have used, material that a lesser dramatist would have considered suitable or even highly effective in its theatrical or rhetorical effects.

If we look at some dozen of such potential scenes that find no place in *Macbeth* we notice at once that not only is the logical continuity of event set aside in some cases but that it is superseded in order that a profound reality may thereby have the greater power to evoke an imaginative response. At the risk of seeming to speak frivolously, I will name some of these, because I think that each one on my list would have been seized

93

on as valuable theatrical material by some Elizabethan drama-tist (even if we have to go as low as Chettle to find him), and that some of them have counterparts easily recognized in the work of the major Jacobeans. Some of these could take the form predominantly of spectacle, some of poetic or rhetorical soliloquy; some again could be built into effective episodes presented through the dialogue.

Shakespeare gives us nothing of the turbulent emotions that must have occupied Macbeth's mind during that ride from Forres to Inverness (between I. iv and I. v) when, with murder in his heart, he rode ahead to provide for Duncan's coming; nor of Lady Macbeth's when, a prey to the same nightmare thoughts, she presided at the supper of Duncan between I. vi and I. vii. Shakespeare does not present the murder of Duncan between II. i and II. ii, nor the coronation of Macbeth between II. iii and III. i. Nor, though he makes clear that there is an in-terval, does he give us any episode to illustrate the first stages of Macbeth's assumption of power, any soliloquy in which Mac-beth should decide upon the murder of Banquo (that crucial decision which separates him from Lady Macbeth), nor that other soliloquy which would have disclosed Macbeth's grow-ing sense of insecurity, so clearly acknowledged in III. i. We have no scene in which he orders the murder of Lady Macduff, comparable to III. i in which he arranges that of Banquo. And when we pass into the later part of the play we find that we have seen nothing of the many further incidents of Macbeth's tyrannous and uneasy reign which are commonplaces to Mal-colm and Macduff in IV. iii. Neither have we any picture of Lady Macbeth's mental progress between the banquet of III. iv and the sleepwalking of V. i; during three scenes she has not appeared at all. There is no record of the mustering of the Eng-lish forces between IV. iii and V. ii, nor of the simultaneous rising of the Scots, and again no revelation of Macbeth's inner experience between IV. i and V. ii, when during three scenes he himself does not appear.

The Nature of Plot in Drama

Now I submit that none of these are impracticable in the theatre. The Elizabethan soliloquy was equal to the revelation of any thought or emotion and though certain of the scenes suggested would have repeated the form of others already in the play, there are contemporaries of Shakespeare who would not have been deterred by this from a fine piece of theatrical effect; any skilled dramatist knows how to vary his repetitions and even to snatch a cumulative effect from them. Furthermore, five at least of these are scenes that few working theatremen who were not great artists would have been likely to resist: the murder of Duncan, the coronation of Macbeth, the haunting of Lady Macbeth's mind by the crimes she has known or guessed at, the mustering of the English army, and the rising of the Scots to join them. It would have been a strangely different play if we had had these instead of or as well as what we have. But it is evident that the scenes that are there must have some superior power of carrying the action from point to point so as to stimulate our imaginations to conceive the whole.

The art of the dramatist has been engaged not in presenting a closely locked and logically coherent action that points irresistibly to a certain deduction, but in selecting those fragments of the whole that stimulate our imaginations to an understanding of the essential experience, to the perception of a nexus of truths too vast to be defined as themes, whose enduring power disengages a seemingly unsending series of perceptions and responses.

It would seem that the imagination of audience or reader is thrown forward, by the immense impact of such scenes, upon a track of emotional experience, to come to rest upon the next scene, at the moment in its curving flight at which it can alight without interference or loss of momentum, to be projected again upon another movement, there to be similarly received, diverted, and flung out again upon its track of discovery. And this proceeds with economy and harmony as do the forces of gravitation at work upon the movements of the bodies in a solar system.

Shakespeare the Dramatist

May we attempt, despite the presumption of the act, to consider, by looking at what goes before and what follows, why Shakespeare does not give us the murder of Duncan? Our imaginations have been engaged first by the fortunes of Macbeth through the initial meeting with the witches and his rapid rise to favour and power and then by the terrible conflict in his mind as temptation lays holds upon it and the vision of murder 'shakes so [his] single state of man that function is smothered in surmise'. From this point we identify ourselves with Macbeth; we have looked into his mind by one of those shafts of illumination which are the glory of the evocative technique in the revelation of character. The meeting with Lady Macbeth at once releases and directs the full force of those elemental powers of evil which lead him forward towards the crime he dreads and desires. From the moment at which he sees the air-drawn dagger he is in a state of suspended life in which time and place and fact have lost their customary relations, in which he sees only 'the future in the instant'. In that world of his imagination, and of ours identified with his, the murder is already done; the act itself is a piece of automatism, a kind of sleepwalking, the mere embodying in deed of what his will and resolution had already accomplished. There is no interim between this and the revulsion and horror which follow immediately after it; almost we may believe that that recoil would have followed if the deed had been imagined only and prevented of actual achievement. In this flight from one point of experience to another there is no room for pause; the presentation of the deed itself would have been a disastrous and irrelevant interruption, breaking the curve of the essential experience. For the act itself which is for Macbeth a timeless interim, a suspension of the faculties, could not have been so for us, the audience. We should have had perforce to subject our imaginations to that scene and in so doing change the swift forward movement of our minds. Even if the dramatist had presented to us a Macbeth who himself moved like a sleep-walker, it would still have been a fatal interruption. And in fact he could hardly have done this if he had lifted the scene into the dominant position it must occupy if it is to be presented at all. For Macbeth in this trance-like frenzy of resolution to have spoken would have been impossible; the silence of suspended consciousness does not speak, even in soliloquy. And yet no such scene as this could have been trusted to dumb show. All other possible stage treatments our fancy can devise lead us but to the same conclusion, that the essential, inner experience which is the essence of the play's action here must move swift as thought from the moment when the bell invites him to the moment when he heard 'a noise' 'as [he] descended'. From the middle of I. iv to the end of II. ii is a 'hideous storm of terror' from which there must be no respite for the audience until, dazed and horror-stricken, we come to rest to hear the intrusion of the everyday world as the porter grumbles his way to the door on which the knocking still resounds.

Such, I would suggest, is the process at work as the action of great poetic drama is embodied in a sequence of events ordered not by demonstrative but by poetic logic. So great is its evocative power that our imagination can bridge a gap which in lesser drama and in common life would contain the crucial event of Macbeth's career. This or a like process will be found to indicate not merely the gaps and the omissions but the functional relations of the moments by which the artist leads us, from point to point, to an apprehension of the essential action of the play which the presentation of outward fact not only could not give us but would in certain instances destroy.

This seemingly arbitrary selection of crucial situations was the customary foundation of Elizabethan drama; the finest tragic dramatists, Marlowe, Webster, Middleton, Ford, all seem to be feeling their way to the same kind of plot as we find in Shakespeare and sometimes triumphantly if intermittently achieving it. The succession of disconnected crises that we sometimes find even in the major and usually in the minor dramatists points to a failure of artistic imagination in them, an imperfect hold upon the action (in Aristotle's sense) by whose direction Shakespeare's plots were unfolded.

*

We spoke at the beginning of this chapter of the inner and outer aspects of the plot and though the distinction is dangerous if it is used arbitrarily, it has a certain value. Some of the events in the plot belong to the surface and we are aware of them at once as deeds or speeches that visibly determine its direction. If we could imagine a sequence of outer events that formed a coherent series in a play we could speak of an outer plot, and if we could be made aware of the corresponding sequence of inner events we could similarly speak of the inner plot. In fact we cannot do either, for we cannot imagine a series sufficiently coherent to form by itself a plot or a strand of a plot, but it is evident that the two processes are at work in every play which is a work of art and that their relative proportions and the interplay between them go far to determine the nature of the play. A play which discloses the deeper levels of experience in the minds of the characters is to that extent concerned with an inner level of plot and one which shows us principally the effects of these experiences is concerned primarily with an outer plot; if Kyd's *Hamlet* had survived (always supposing it to have existed) it would, we may suppose, be found to have treated the story in such a way that the proportions and relations of these two aspects of its plot were like those of *The Spanish Tragedy*. But these are not the proportions or the relations of Shakespeare's *Hamlet*.

A plot which leaves upon our minds the impression that it is logical, argumentative, or demonstrative will be found to be so at its outer as at its inner level and a play whose structure is evocative will be so at both levels also. I have already suggested [1] that in *Macbeth* an event or series of events may evoke

[1] p. 97.

The Nature of Plot in Drama

in our imaginations other intervening events, so that we pass from one to another without the sense of hiatus or space and end with a sense of the continuity of the whole, ordered sequence. Just so, the revelation of inner event may proceed in this way, whether by soliloquy or by dialogue. Macbeth's soliloquy 'If it were done when 'tis done', although it begins as an attempt to think out his position, is filled with thick-coming fancies and terrifying images that seem to leave his argument where it began. But we who have heard him know that a long phase of experience has been lived through and the very pauses, changes of direction, or inconsistencies have but shown us the journeying mind coming momentarily into sight. They have evoked in our imaginations the experience through which he has travelled; but it is an experience of which much is left undescribed, even in soliloquy. So it is with Hamlet when he sets out to debate whether to be or not to be. Our imaginations leap the gaps with his. The inner plot here uses its own special medium of revelation, the soliloquy, but the mode is still evocative, even within the soliloquy itself. The progress of a mind intent upon its inner experience may be revealed to us by just such a stirring of our imaginations when Lear speaks to the Fool in Act I, scene v. We no longer see the same man at the end of that short passage of dialogue as we did at the beginning; we have followed the slender but sufficient clues through a wilderness of experience and self-discovery.

In the same way, we may recognize the contrary mode; the logical treatment of plot that we find in *The Alchemist* or *Strife* may be discovered also at the inner level whenever the experience of a character is revealed systematically, step by step; so that, whatever its relation to the events that belong primarily to the outer aspect of the plot, we recognize a piece of continuous disclosure or self-discovery going on beneath that surface. This is comparatively rare in drama, but we may find it in Racine's *Bérénice* or *Athalie* and we find it again in Ibsen's *Rosmersholm* or *John Gabriel Borkman*. Rebekka West, like Mrs

Alving, has made a great part of her pilgrimage before the play opens, but *Rosmersholm*, unlike *Ghosts*, is mainly concerned with the final stages of her interpretation, with her assessment of her past conduct, and her deliberate translation of her final decision into action. And her mind, despite the strength of her emotions, works as clearly upon the true meaning of her past and the dilemma it has created in the present as if she were examining the motives and conduct of another person. Our imagination is required to follow her steps, but not to leap chasms with her.

Some indication of the variety possible to the inter-relations of these different levels of plot may be seen when we look at Ibsen's play bearing in mind such a play as *Hamlet* where also the inner aspect is concerned with exploration, a measure of self-discovery and integration. In *Hamlet*, the events in the world that surrounds him continually affect and are in turn affected by his inward progression; neither escapes for long the influence of the other. But in plays such as *Rosmersholm* the events that make up the surface become a mere vehicle for the significant succession of inner events. Moreover, this drama arises primarily not from the effect of tragic or catastrophic event upon the surface level of the play or from entirely new experience offered by this to the character, but from exploration and revaluation of the past in the light of these events, of fresh situations and changing relations. The material for an Elizabethan domestic tragedy does indeed lie behind the play; a long history of mingled events upon both levels, of interesting deeds, thoughts and decisions has brought the characters to the point at which they now stand. But the substance of the play itself is the recollection of that history and the re-assessment both of it and of the present to which Rebekka is prompted by the slight and relatively colourless surface events of the play.[1]

[1] The unfailing tact of the Greek drama leads to its special rendering by the aid of the Chorus of the relationship between the levels of event. The

The Nature of Plot in Drama

Some relation between these levels, between that which lies upon the surface and that which lies at varying depths beneath it, reveals itself then as surely in a play's structure as in the dramatist's revelation of character. But equally surely the mode of the essential dramatist distinguishes itself in both from that of the philosophic dramatist. And the mark of the evocative mode is, even here, its generic power, while the mark of the other is its logical demonstration. Even in so great a play as *Rosmersholm*, where the poetry of Ibsen's thought creates high imaginative drama, the logic of inner event is still to be found in the process of the mind which is revealed at the inner level of the plot.

From the linking and proportioning of these two levels comes, as I have suggested, the balance of the play's content. From their separation many significant implications derive. One of these in Elizabethan drama is the impression of the fluidity of time and of the different nature which it may assume at different moments. Our sense of multiple time-schemes within a play such as *Othello* comes in part from this difference of the tempo, the inner life proceeding with a swiftness perfectly consistent with common experience, the succession of outer events occupying meanwhile a brief space of solar time. The systole and diastole of many plays may be traced to the same cause; two separate and equally true ways of measuring time, implied by the two different levels, may reveal at the heart of a play a hint of the mystery of the two lives led by every man, of the mystery, that is, of incarnation.

---

disclosure of the characters' motives and reflections gives us the origins of their actions, but the acts themselves are banished from the stage. Thus we have a drama which lays emphasis upon the inner aspect of plot in the midst of tragic and catastrophic outward events. These events are withdrawn into the background and the causes and responses within the human soul are given their true supremacy.

101

VI

Communication in Thought

WE HAVE LOOKED FIRST at a dramatist at work upon the revelation of character and on the ordered sequence of events that make the plot because these are the aspects of the play to which we turn first when we are thinking about the dramatic mode. They make up the greater part of the play's content; the greater part – but not all. There remains the language itself, forming yet another aspect of the play's technique and as evidently bringing its own contribution to the total effect; the sound or the immediate sense of words considered singly or in small groups, perhaps afterwards to be related together in their proper and continuous pattern, words in their own right, distinguishable from their function as mediators of the content. All this will be found in a work of art to be in harmony with the mode already discovered in the treatment of character and plot. There remains above all the imagery, which is a special part of this and sometimes, as in the visual imagery called for by settings, almost a separable part and self-contained.

But between them, at this point, there comes into sight another factor, neither wholly a matter of character nor wholly of plot and yet not definable simply in terms of the language which clothes it and them, difficult to define and still more difficult to name and yet undoubtedly playing its part in great drama (an aggressive part in some) and again claiming consideration in its own right. There are speeches whose function is not solely that of furthering event or revealing character or even both of these; speeches which sometimes reveal, in

Communication in Thought

our final image of the play, too consistent and too continuous a nature of their own to be judged merely as an element of the plot or the property of any one character. Their contribution to the play appears to be a part, but not the whole, of what Aristotle called *dianoia*; under due safeguards it is possible to speak of it in English as thought.

When Ulysses in *Troilus and Cressida* describes at length in the Greek camp the nature of 'degree' or of the hierarchical state,[1] when Hector a little later [2] debates with the Trojans the nature of value, the form of the dialogue is an argument, the subject-matter is an idea or a group of related ideas, the force which makes speech vivid and vehement is a passionate absorption in the experience of thinking; the passages contribute less to the ordered sequence of events in the play, for indeed neither passage affects the immediate movement of event, than to the revelation of the ideas, preconceptions or assumptions on which the play rests, the intellectual motives which were part of the characters' passion from the beginning, part of the initial action of the play. Thinking, for such characters, is passionate experience and we recognize this when we respond to these scenes as to any other essentially dramatic passage or episode. We meet the same kind of material in the English history plays, and especially in the two parts of *Henry IV*, and something akin to it in the comparatively rare instances of serious debate in soliloquy such as those of Claudius and Angelo. Wherever we find this emphasis upon argument or self-examination, upon the process we speak of as 'thinking it out', we meet in effect an emphasis laid upon one side of human experience; and if a large proportion of the play's content is of this kind (as it is in *Troilus and Cressida*) we find an exceptional grouping or selection of characters who are themselves prone to or apt for that experience. This proneness to thought (or 'thinking'), when, so far from being out of character, it is of the very essence of the characters' natures and part of their

[1] *T.C.* I. iii. 83-134.   [2] *T.C.* II. ii.

passionate experience, is undeniably dramatic and it is what we mean by 'thought' in drama. After what we have already said [in previous chapters] we shall be prepared to find that, in the various dramatists' treatment of this element of the play, there is room again for diversity of mode.

We have been using the word 'thought' until now without strict definition, but it is advisable to bear in mind the most frequent connotations of the word in a dramatic context. If we begin by speaking of a single character, we may mean by his thought the process or method of his thinking, revealed as part of his experience (and so fit matter for drama).[1] Or we may think of the conclusions he draws, at whatever level of consciousness, from this process and this too will be part of his experience and so again fit matter for drama. But we may, if we wish, think of the characters collectively instead of individually and here again we shall need the word 'thought' to describe the effect on the tone and mood of the play of the thinking contained in it, of the total activity of thinking, of the sum of all the characters' experience of that process. And again, as with the individual character, we may mean by 'thought' the total body of ideas expressed, the sum of the conclusions of all the characters. For certain dramatists and in certain plays, we may add a fifth and a sixth connotation, using the term 'thought' to mean the process of thinking or the resultant conclusions of the dramatist himself. When this is made unmistakeably clear, when, that is to say, we hear the voice of the dramatist in addition to that of his character, when we recognize the ideas of Chapman extending beyond or even conflicting with those of Byron or Bussy, we are disconcerted and perceive that we are no longer assisting at a play. We have emerged momentarily from the dramatic into some other mode. This is not Shakespeare's way, nor that of any wholly dramatic writer, for it is as unnatural (and as unnecessary) for

[1] 'Fit matter for drama' does not, of course, imply that the matter is necessarily used dramatically in any given passage or by any given dramatist.

Communication in Thought

him to present his ideas as abstract principles within his play as
for the painter or musician to resort to words instead of to his
own medium. We may, it is true, apprehend something of his
underlying ideas about life from the total body of his art or
even from a single work, but we make this abstraction ourselves and the process is a complex one. No single character, not
Ulysses, not Henry IV on his death-bed, gives us Shakespeare's
idea of the nature of kingship or government, for each gives us
strictly and dramatically his own inference from his own experience. That the experience of each of these comes near to
Shakespeare's imaginative experience of the same situation we
may conjecture, but that neither coincides precisely with the
implications of the total body of the Histories we may see for
ourselves if we make the empirical test of taking either speech
as a gloss upon that whole body. The individuality of the
speaker deflects it at one point or another; it is no true epitome
of the thought that underlies all those plays, from *Henry VI*
to *The Tempest*, which contain characters concerned with this
theme.[1]

[1] It would be convenient if we could say that 'thought', in so far as it is
fit matter for drama, was covered by Aristotle's term 'dianoia', but in fact
there is overlapping, but not coincidence. To accept Butcher's assumption
(*Aristotle and the Fine Arts* (ed. 1923) p. 337, n. 2, quoting R. P. Hardie in
Mind, vol. IV, No. 15) that by 'διάνοια' Aristotle did in fact mean 'μίμησις
τῆς διανοίας', without providing this aspect of technique with a special term
to delimit the relationship, as he did with μῦθος and πρᾶξις, is to exclude
satisfactorily enough the directly revealed thought of the dramatist and to
confine the use of the term to the first four connotations that we have
suggested, to the thought, that is, of the character or characters. But even so,
the last two of these would appear to fall outside the content of Aristotle's
'dianoia' (*Poetics*, VI, 6, 16, 17) and the first two (or, indeed, all four) to
contain rather less than is required by *Poetics*, XIX, 2, or *Ethics*, VI, 2. We
must therefore reluctantly abandon what looks at first like a convenient
category and continue to lay the burden of differentiation upon our own
overworked term, 'thought'.

Again, it may be questioned why Aristotle did not warn us against the

Shakespeare the Dramatist

But there are, as we have said, certain plays in which the element of thought, while being essentially dramatic, forms a large part of the content and others again in which we suspect that its intrusion is not entirely dramatic. In the first case, we find a drama in which thought preponderates to such a degree as to outweigh or to threaten other interests suggesting a different kind of drama from anything we have hitherto considered. In the second, we shall probably find that the play falls short of the essential dramatic mode. And in both we must be prepared to distinguish its functions in relation to character and to plot.[1]

The most interesting plays thus weighted with thought are found in modern drama, from that phase, that is to say, which begins with Shakespeare and leads up to Ibsen and his successors, not because thought is alien to Greek drama but because the presence of the chorus there alters the balance of distribution.[2] The most evident speeches of this kind are perhaps those which present conclusions; adjudications, summaries of a position reached at the end of a process of thinking which is

---

danger of preoccupation with dianoia as he did against the danger of neglecting muthos for ethos. This answer is simply that dianoia is the active principle in character and ethos the passive groundwork of personality. So, while it is quite possible (see below) to find plays unduly given to 'thought' in the sense in which we are here using the term, a play unduly given to dianoia at the expense of muthos would be a contradiction in terms. This again serves to mark the distinction between dianoia and 'thought' (as used here) and between the aspects of dramatic content which they define.

[1] It is evident from the outset that no limit is set by the nature of drama to the extent to which thinking and thought may become part of the content of a play. For obviously no subject-matter can be inherently undramatic if it is possible to human nature to make of it a passionate experience.

[2] The Greek dramatists were for the most part able to transfer to the chorus the task of presenting the final impression of and conclusions from the thought of all the characters ('thought' III and IV), thus securing its presentation without laying this responsibility upon the dialogue.

Communication in Thought

not itself presented. They are such speeches as are made in everyday life by a judge or a chairman of a board, and often contain a statement of relevant theory or a definition of policy. The sequence of the parts or the shape of the argument is, as a rule, undisturbed by emotion; the speaker's emotion, if any, is controlled and that of the hearers is revealed chiefly by implication in the preceding or following speeches and events. Such is the speech in which Claudius addresses his court at the beginning of *Hamlet*,[1] a state-speech, a public declaration of policy, a ministerial report. Such, too, though delivered in the form of soliloquy, is Prince Henry's comment on his Eastcheap associates,[2] a piece not of thinking but of recapitulation, whose conclusions are clear and definite and evidently long familiar. So, too, in the main, is the death-bed speech of Henry IV,[3] which, despite the controlled emotion which gives it power, is essentially reminiscent of earlier thought, a distillation of the wisdom brought by bitter experience and endorsed 'like deep harmony' by the tongue of a dying man. And such again is the speech of the Lord Chief Justice later in the play,[4] the definition at once of his position and his creed, an orderly exposition undisturbed either by his own underlying emotion or the tension of the situation. We may add to these Ulysses's speech[5] on the hierarchical State and the consequences of the Greek neglect of degree, a long and masterly statement of a theory of government applied to a specific crisis. His thoughts do not arise in his mind as he speaks: they are the fruit of long-considered policy, prepared beforehand and delivered, as they should be, with vigour but without confusion. All these are essentially dramatic because, though not a revelation of passionate thinking, they are the consequences in one form or other of thought that has been evoked by passion and because they are either the cause or consequence of passionate event. They rightly have the

[1] *Hamlet*, I. ii. 1–39.   [2] I *Henry IV*, I. iii. 217–39.
[3] II *Henry IV*, IV. v. 180–218.   [4] II *Henry IV*, V. ii. 73–101.
[5] *Troilus and Cressida*, I. iii. 83–134.

appearance of impersonal deliveries because they are spoken by men trained by office to deliver impersonal judgements upon momentous occasions and led or forced to do so here by the surrounding events. We may add to these one or two other speeches, conceived and delivered in the same mood in response to the same demands: Athena's verdict at the end of the *Eumenides*, the judgement of Tullius at the end of *Horace*,[1] or Cinna's speeches[2] on the nature of the Roman nation and its government. The list could be extended.

When we come to consider the exchange of thought in discussion, we are on rather different ground. The same laws govern argument or debate as govern all revelation of thought in drama, but the process of thinking appears side by side with the results in the speeches of at least some of the characters and, if the issue be vital enough to be fit matter for drama, emotion is likely to find its way into expression. Much of such dialogue is like the speech of counsel rather than the judge's summing up, the cabinet debate rather than the ministerial pronouncement. It attempts to reach a conclusion or to convince its dramatic audience and it is more usually a passage of dialogue than a single speech.[3] Such are the debate on war policy in the Trojan council chamber,[4] which resolves itself into a close discussion of the nature of value or the rougher and less keenly analytical discussion of conduct and policy between Westmorland, Mowbray, and the Archbishop of York.[5] Such also are, in effect if not in fact, three scenes in which the form of a discussion is maintained and in two of which passionate concern is simulated, though in fact the underlying purposes of the disputants are quite other. The first is Henry V's discussion with

---

[1] *Horace*, V. iii. [2] *Cinna*, II. i. 145–67, 215–306.
[3] As a single speech we may instance that of the Bishop of Carlisle (*Richard II*, IV. i. 114–19). This stands alone simply because it is met not by a counter-argument but by his arrest.
[4] *Troilus and Cressida*, II. ii.
[5] II *Henry IV*, IV. i. (the whole scene).

Communication in Thought

his advisors on the interpretation of Salique law,[1] where the actual and perhaps the dramatic audience suspects that his intention is not so much to discover the truth as to provide himself with an excuse, and the discussion lacks urgency because the conclusion is predetermined. Another and subtler use of an argument concealing rather than declaring the intentions of the debaters is that in which Richard of Gloucester [2] stages his mock-refusal of the crown and his hypocritical capitulation. Some close and cunning argument is here reproduced both by Richard and Buckingham, but the scene derives its dramatic power less from the passion with which the argument is pursued than from the continual conflict between the debating points adduced and the known intentions of the two chief characters. The apparent debate, in which the processes of thinking are simulated, is well-enough reasoned to give it dramatic interest, but that interest is heightened by the irony and by passions that move not within the thought but beneath its deceptive surface. Not unlike this is the opening scene of the second act of *Cinna*, where the debate on imperial rule between Augustus, Cinna, and Maximus has also two levels of meaning. But here the arguments for and against Augustus's policy, though clearly enough worked out, are hardly urgent enough to hold our interest. Nor can they be, for, not only are they again simulated argument, but we are much more deeply engaged upon a series of more urgent questions as to who is in fact deceiving whom and whether or not some sudden disclosure is to be made. But all these scenes are built out of thought and out of the preoccupation of the speakers with their own thought whether revealed or concealed, and in all of them we watch the process of thinking, at one or at two levels, and the thinking and the thought are the dramatic substance of the scene.

Of a different kind again is self-examination as often as this takes or attempts to take the form of a debate in the mind of the speaker; the process then is that of thinking out his position

[1] *Henry V*, I. ii. 1–114.   [2] *Richard III*, III. vii. 116–72.

109

or intentions and not an expression of feeling alone. The normal form for this is soliloquy which, at least among the Elizabethans and in some degree until the coming of naturalism, represents, by an agreed convention, the unspoken thought of a character. It is indeed possible for a character to conduct his self-examination in a speech or speeches which are made to another person and yet primarily précis of genuine thinking aloud. But such speeches are in fact extremely rare, as is indeed the situation in which they could occur.[1] Nor can we include in this group all soliloquies for not all soliloquies reveal a process which reaches by argument a conclusion, valid or false, upon which action is or is to be based. The diversity within this group is very great, for here the whole range of the mind may be revealed, its individual processes of thinking followed without constraint; there is no dramatic audience for the speaker to persuade or convince and to whom he must adapt his expression and the steps of his reasoning. Moreover, in this kind of speech, the relationship between emotion and thought becomes more intricate. Thought itself may be of passionate intensity, it is true, but it is also true that in many soliloquies, even where

[1] Most of these resolve themselves upon inspection into summaries of conclusions already reached or into debates in which the other character supplies from time to time opposition or encouragement and so gives a fresh direction to the thought. Self-examination in the presence of another character is not unspoken thought but confession and though there is nothing to prevent this being a process of 'thinking things out', the situation is rare in life and still more rarely part of a dramatic sequence of events. Ibsen probably brings us nearer to it than any other dramatist.

It is clearly among the moderns that we must look for it and there only in realistic drama. For wherever the soliloquy is an accepted convention, it is unnecessary and the use of it will probably reveal a mistaken conception on the part of the dramatist as to the processes by which the character could have explored his own mind. Corneille's *Polyeucte* seems to offer an instance of this, in the scene (III. v) in which Félix analyses in the presence of Albin the effects of an experience too recent for us to suppose that he could yet have reached clear conclusions upon it. (See above p. 44.)

Communication in Thought

thought is dominant and the thinker determined to organize his experience to reach a conclusion, the very depth of his concern with his thinking may itself interfere with the process; the emotions which arise at each step may cross it and disturb the orderly procedure that was his intention. In Claudius's prayer,[1] in the two passages of Angelo's self-examination,[2] there is hardly a trace of the detachment maintained by Henry IV or by the Lord Chief Justice, even in the midst of tension. In such self-communing the 'whirl-wind of passion' contends with the stillness of ordered thought, but not to its complete disordering. This is essential to any faithful and dramatic revelation of passionate thinking in soliloquy and Shakespeare's characters, from Proteus[3] to Prospero,[4] confirm this truth. For if, in any comparable situation, the logical form and the detachment is preserved that was proper to character and situation when Ulysses spoke or Henry IV, we are uneasily aware of something which is not a revelation of human experience in the mind of the character before us, but a summary of conclusions which could only have been reached at some psychological distance from the event; the thought has been unnaturally rescued from the turmoil of emotion and set out as an ordered sequence whose very brevity and coherence put it outside the world of the drama before us and constitute a narrative summary of a part of its inner plot. This convention, for a convention it sometimes is, is the reverse of that by which soliloquy admits us to the inner thought of a character; instead it puts us at two removes from his experience of the moment and gives us the likeness of that experience, robbed of its immediacy, as it may perhaps be destined to appear to him at some later date or in a future beyond the play. Such doubts extend to many impressive speeches in the plays of Corneille; to Emilie's in the opening

[1] *Hamlet*, III. iii. 36–72.
[2] *Measure for Measure*, II. ii. 161–87 and II. iv. 1–17.
[3] *Two Gentlemen of Verona*, II. v. 193–215; II. vi. 1–43.
[4] *The Tempest*, V. i. 33–57.

soliloquy of *Cinna*, to Pauline's at the beginning of the third act of *Polyeucte*, to Félix's in a passage already spoken of a little later in that same act.[1] But when the characters of Racine, on the other hand, set themselves to think out their problems, they so think and feel that the very process of their thinking and feeling rises, as does that of Shakespeare's characters, before our eyes.[2] Among the dramatists of the nineteenth century none has this secret more surely than Ibsen, whose Brand, a man whose profession compels self-examination as an exercise, carries us with him step by step through his agonized progress to conclusions which are but half-truths.[3] And beside him, in at least one speech, is Bjørnson's Paul Lange.[4]

It has already been implied that among the dramatists I have instanced, it is Corneille who appears to work in another and perhaps less dramatic mode in this matter of revealing the process of thinking and in the relation in his works between the process and the resultant thought. And since thought, both as thoughts and as thinking, is a great part of his subject-matter, it is clear that he presents us with something which must either distinguish him from most other dramatists or lead us to revise our conclusions. For one could no more dispute the importance of argument and debate in his dialogue and soliloquy than one could deny the predominance of characters in his plays whose minds are alive with thought and who reflect its habit in the very rhythm and syntax of their speeches and in their compensating paucity of imagery.

The glory of Corneille's drama lies precisely in this, that it is a drama of thought. The characters exist to express it and the structure to sustain it. It is found in its most stirring form in the

[1] *Polyeucte*, III. v. 12–28.
[2] As, for instance, the soliloquies of Antiochus (*Bérénice*, I. ii), Titus (ibid., IV. iv), Atalide (*Bajazet*, V. i), Mithridate (*Mithridate*, IV. v), to indicate only a few.
[3] See especially *Brand*, Acts I, IV, and V.
[4] *Paul Lange and Tora Parsburg* (V.).

Communication in Thought

plays in which the characters deliberate least, in which thought or thinking is less a matter of reflection than of swift balancing of conflicting codes or duties and of equally swift decisions rapidly calculated from the results of a parallelogram of psychological forces. The pace and the passion of drama are to be found in the clash between love and hate on the one hand and iron discipline of an accepted code of honour and conduct upon the other. Provided only that this is the kind of code that human beings may create and that they know their responses by heart, one does not question the processes of their thought or the mode of revelation. One knows them only too well. Their codes may be primitive but they are clear and they are gallant. And the type of character, above all others, to whom this is natural is the soldier.

When, therefore, Corneille fills his plays with soldiers and the women bred in the tradition of the services, he gives us a play that satisfies our instinctive demands upon drama and will prove upon examination to satisfy such dramatic laws as we are able to discern. It is not for nothing Le Cid has entranced readers and audiences of many races who are slow to respond to certain of his other plays. For a soldier's honour is a real thing and a part of everyday existence wherever survival depends upon the valour and the power of leadership that only unflawed honour can give. This play lives by virtue of the mood of high excitement, brilliant with passion and torment and the supreme vitality of youth. And so long as the play is filled with the very people, the young and the men dedicated to the military code, in whom such swift and passionate action is native in response to their code, so long is the play dramatic. They are men for whom 'it were an easy leap To pluck bright honour from the pale-faced moon', and had Shakespeare written a play peopled only with Hotspurs and Sewards, it might have resembled this. Only, Shakespeare would never so have peopled his play. And this indicates a gulf between the two dramatists which may be found to reach to the foundations of dramatic art. Moreover, his Hotspurs are maculate and imperfect beings while the Rodrigues must of necessity be as immaculate as Galahad; one sees the shining of the silver armour and hears the high, clear clash of its movements as the noble lines ring down upon the stage.

But where, when we have admitted this, is the thought in that stricter kind which is characteristic of Cornelian drama? The characters even here think out each position as it confronts them, balance the alternatives, reject one with passionate regret but select and act swiftly upon the other. And in doing this they explain their motives or that part of their motive which has been indoctrinated in them by the code. And their explanation is a calculation of conflicting claims natural only to a certain military caste trained so to calculate and to decide by established criteria without reference to and if necessary in defiance of the deep-lying instincts, of the promptings that rise from the inner experience or the total consciousness, and so affords us perhaps the only instance possible of a self-explanatory character which is yet a mediator of drama. When all is said, these men search not their hearts but the code which tells them how to act without reference to the heart. This may afford a noble theme, but it is not in effect a part of common human experience; it is so far from universal that what is distinctive in it is scarcely human, though it may be universally accepted as the superhuman achievement of dedicated men. In short, in the one play in which Corneille writes what is indubitably drama in a widely accepted kind and creates that drama out of thought, he does this precisely by specializing the type of character and the type of thinking within extremely narrow limits. Within these limits he has succeeded, to the extent of one play, of making the reasoned debate the substance of his play and that substance dramatic. He appears to leave us face to face with the astonishing paradox that only men of action, in action, can reason dramatically.

It is his other plays then that afford us what we are seeking, a drama in which the characters reason and debate with each other and with themselves at the crucial moments of the plot, in which there is a continuous attempt to reveal their inner experience to us largely in terms of deduction and of self-explanation. It is a drama, in which the reasoning process seems to be idealized as at once the object of aspiration and the means of moral achievement. Such a drama is naturally peopled with beings for whom reason holds a high place in the scale of aids and means to virtue, who seek to solve perplexity by reference not to the hidden depths of their being but to the clear and burnished surface of consciousness. It is habitual with such persons to approach a crisis with a clear intention to think out where they stand before they go further: 'Settle thy studies, Faustus, and begin/To sound the depth of that thou wilt profess.' But neither they nor Faustus at this point of his experience do in fact sound those depths, for the intention in both cases is to pass in review the conflicting desires or purposes and to act upon a deduction that follows from that survey. We are not concerned here with the question of whether persons with a persistent habit of self-explanation and self-analysis may exist, but with the question of whether, if they do, they are fit subjects for drama. If their reasoning is other than a swift and vehement comparison of conflicting codes and an equally swift and soldierly choice between them, then it is likely, as we have suggested, to be the result of a fixed habit of inward, philosophical debate. And if the process and demeanour which properly result from this are suffered to determine the form of their expression at moments which the dramatist claims to be those of intense emotion, then either the emotion is not in fact intense, in which case their philosophical demeanour can well be a faithful picture of human conduct, or he has falsified their experience by causing them to display a philosophic demeanour impossible to passionate men in the grip of their passions. In the first instance the character, being predominantly dispassionate, is unfit matter for drama and in the second the falsification of character, together with the remoteness superimposed upon its

Shakespeare the Dramatist

expression, destroys the cogency and the immediacy of drama. We are driven to conclude that conditions such as those of *Le Cid* are the only ones in which self-expression in the form of reasoned exposition at the moments of emotional crisis can appear natural to 'man doing and suffering', and that in conditions that lack the peculiar kind of urgency and pressure proper to this play, the habit appears to misrepresent the normal processes of human behaviour.

This leads us immediately to another question. Have we in fact grounds for concluding that the matter of thought may itself be so treated by one dramatist as to be essentially dramatic and by another as to be in certain respects undramatic? Is there in fact a dramatic mode of revealing thought and an undramatic mode of presenting it? Does Corneille, for instance, fall into an undramatic mode by the unnatural completeness of expression that he imposes on the characters.[1]

What holds our attention, then? In what is it that we are interested, in the characteristic Cornelian drama, that drama in which thought is a high activity explicitly expressed and proceeding at the surface of the characters' minds? To answer this fairly we must look at passages which are part of the poet's intention, led up to by preceding scenes, placed and timed with precision and built into the play.[2] Such a scene is that, already

[1] In so far as the reasoning being has full right to reason in a play, provided he does so with passionate intensity, we may instance many of Ibsen's people, notably Brand and Mrs Alving, in each of whom the habit is justified by circumstance or training. What Ibsen does not do is to fill his play with such characters on the one hand or to let them explain themselves in defiance of their nature and habits on the other. Given a world whose Autolycuses were reasonable and whose Dogberries lucid we should have to admit the universality of the reasoning habit. But we should still be free to maintain that that habit, dispassionately prevailing, did not afford to its poets matter for that form of art that we call drama.

[2] Not, that is to say, scenes which appear (as does *Macbeth* IV. i) to change the tempo of the play, to arrest movement and to puzzle criticism by appearing as eddies or backwaters of the main-stream of the drama.

Communication in Thought

referred to, which opens the second act of *Cinna*, where for some 250 lines, the three characters on the stage engage in a long debate on the advantages and disadvantages of imperial and democratic government, although the purpose of the argument is not in fact to arrive at a decision on that issue nor to lead on through that decision to some determining events in inner or outer plot. For this scene rests on a basis of irony and derives its suspense not from the direction or conclusion of the argument but from the direction and conclusion of a battle of wits to which this is a mask. At both levels it is an intellectual exercise and the fact that is two-fold does not alter the fact that our interest is in the astute, Machiaevellian game of wits and not, as in the superficially similar scene in *Richard III*,[1] in the subtle study of hypocrisy and the imaginative dread which the ominous exercise of Richard's skill evokes.

Augustus has summoned Cinna and Maximus at the height of their conspiracy and as the scene opens we await in suspense, if we are reading the play for the first time, the answer to two questions. Has Augustus discovered the conspiracy or not? Will he or will he not have the two conspirators arrested and executed? These are followed immediately by a third question, as Augustus dismisses his guards and remains alone with the conspirators: will they seize the opportunity to kill him? As the dialogue goes on, our minds are further exercised by trying to discover whether he is in earnest when he asks for their advice on his proposed resignation or whether he is setting a trap for them which, like Henry V with Cambridge, Grey, and Scroop,[2] he will presently spring. As the scene goes on, and it begins to look as though nothing is going to happen from Augustus's side, we give our minds more and more to the underlying ironies, which are themselves subject to doubt from our still unanswered questions. Supposing Augustus to be ignorant of the conspiracy, there is much irony in his asking advice on his position from precisely the two men who have sworn to

[1] *Richard III*, III. vii.   [2] *Henry V*, II. ii.

117

assassinate him, in Cinna's well-argued assurances that his reign is beneficent, when we know that it is Augustus's seizing of the empire that is Cinna's reason for the intended assassination, in Maximus's equally well-argued entreaties that he should resign, when resignation would save him from their vengeance, in the lively and vigorous debate between these two conspirators who are sworn to agreement in a purpose opposite to their words, in the surprise which, though it is concealed until the following scene, we know that each must be feeling at the position taken up by the other. There is excitement in this and the suspense at first reading or hearing is intense; in later readings we must forgo the suspense and depend for enjoyment upon the neatness of the debate and the ironic undertones. But what are we to say of a key scene in which, in all subsequent readings, we are left to depend upon the cunning of the arguments and their ironic implications? That part of suspense which depends on our ignorance of event vanishes also after one reading of *Oedipus* or *Othello*, of any tragedy by a Greek or an Elizabethan dramatist; indeed this ignorance is for most of us like Ann Oldham's virginity, we cannot remember when we lost it. But with the Greeks and the Elizabethans, when that part of suspense is gone which was strictly the province of melodrama, we are left to our imaginative participation in that more terrible suspense which the characters themselves experience. We know how *Macbeth* will end, but that is nothing beside the fact that we are ourselves Macbeth and that he does not. It is the characters and their fates, and the significance of fate and character that engage us here. But Corneille is using certain of the methods of comedy in tragedy – a fact that no one knew better than he[1] – but they are of a specialized kind of comedy, of the kind that watches the manoeuvres of Face and Surface like the evolution of a well-known ballet, for sheer delight in the precision and virtuosity of the movements. It is not the comedy

[1] See *Discours de l'utilité et des parties du poëme dramatique* in *Oeuvres* (1910), I, pp. 13–51, especially p. 30.

Communication in Thought

which holds its breath while Dogberry and Verges obscure urgent police messages or catches that breath when Beatrice cries, 'Kill Claudio!' The scene in *Cinna* that we are watching is no more the comedy of sympathy than it is the tragedy of sympathy and while comedy without good will is possible for a time (but not possible throughout, even for Ben Jonson or for Congreve)[1] tragedy which for any reason hinders the participation of the audience in the experience of the agents thwarts its own purposes. The reason for this is probably to be sought, as we have suggested, in the level of consciousness at which the characters enter upon the conflict. The drama which Kames denounced and about which even Voiture had his doubts [2] reveals, if only by its facility in debate, that we are not assisting at a conflict of the soul.[3]

Thought may indeed be activated by passion and it may then, as in *Le Cid* and in *Faustus*, sometimes become passionate thought, but the areas in which it can operate are extremely small and the boundaries of that area themselves serve to define the dramatic use of thought (always potential matter for drama) and the undramatic deployment of it in debate. For debate is, after all, a small part of total human experience, normal in unusual degree only to certain temperaments, professions, and situations, and though these themselves are as fit matter for drama as anything else, only the passionate part of even that thinking is fit. Mental conflict may indeed rise to the surface as mental debate, but an essential difference exists between the kind of drama in which mingled passion and thought result in

[1] Still less for Plautus or Molière, and, less still again, for Terence. Corneille himself in his comedies comes nearer to it than any of the three, though a twinge of anxiety follows Dorante at his most difficult moments which is not given to the baser villainies of Ben Jonson's criminals.

[2] 'On ne débite pas les lieux communs quand on est profondément ému.'

[3] Preoccupation with this facility may betray the dramatist into an imperfect relation between the conduct of a character and its effects as it does, I think, with Corneille's Félix in *Polyeucte*.

mingled coherence and incoherence, in mingled deed and speech, and the kind in which the thinking and its conclusions, in perfect lucidity and poise, are the main activity of the speakers and the main interest of the hearer. We may attend a trial from concern for and interest in the contestants or we may attend in order to savour the skill of the pleading and of the judge's summing up; it is doubtful whether we can do both in the same instance, and this indicates the gulf between the two attitudes. The same distinction may be drawn between the drama of experience and the drama of debate, with this difference that the second of these attempts to merge prosecutor with plaintiff, defence with defendant; and if the issues are serious our common experience of human behaviour rebels against superimposition of lucid detachment upon passionate concern. The drama of cabinet meetings, council chambers, lecture platforms, and pulpits (except in the rare instances where these issues are matters of life and death), where nothing is confused and little entirely secret, is separated by a wide gulf from the drama that depends upon secret impressions, where the hidden processes of the mind mingle with every stage of argument and help to determine every deed.[1]

[1] A brief comparison with the methods of the Greek dramatists may help to clear up the distinction I have attempted to draw. A Greek dramatist had two ways of conveying the thought of his characters, in their own speeches and in the choric odes. The first is now used, as by the Elizabethans, to an extent and in a context normal and natural to 'man doing and suffering'. For the second, the Elizabethans had no resource but the soliloquy, except in a few passages where they lay upon certain characters, in defiance of dramatic probability, some of the responsibilities of a commentator; Webster and Chapman use most often this undramatic device. But Corneille, having little or no chorus, appears to have transferred this part of its function to the characters themselves, charging them indiscriminately with the burden of thought carried by the Greek chorus. This led to some astonishing results to the balance of character and the consequent veracity of the drama, for the characters must then reveal that part of their hidden reflections

Communication in Thought

Finally, to return to our original question, is it true to say that the thought which forms part of the tissue of a play's content may, like character, be treated in widely differing ways by different dramatists and those the ways of secret impressions upon the one hand and, at the opposite extreme, of less wholly dramatic and more explicit expression? To the first part of this we have already suggested an answer. What we have now to ask is whether thought, in the sense in which we have spoken of it in this chapter, can itself be the vehicle of secret impressions and serve the purposes of evocative drama? We may arrive at some conclusion by comparing Pauline's soliloquy, which opens the third act of *Polyeucte*, with those two in which Angelo finds himself 'that way going to temptation,/Where prayers cross'.[1]

Both are pictures of mental conflict, the first concerned with the conflict of others, the second with its own; but both are alike in recognizing confusion and turmoil, the first of hopes and fears, the second of the 'prayers' that 'cross', and in knowing that out of these some kind of order must be brought. At that point all likeness stops and the significant differences begin. Pauline recognizes the confusion and describes it clearly in lines whose syntax, internal rhythms, and rhyming couplets add precision to every stage of her description.

---

which the Greek chorus had revealed for the Greek dramatists. This lifts the hidden up into explicit expression in an unnatural way and leaves the characters to reveal what they did not know and had no business to know and that in a way which can only be tolerated by the audience if it is revealed by means of a frank convention like the Elizabethan soliloquy and that only when the soliloquy represents thought as it would appear to an audience that could dispense with the medium of words. This constitutes one of the most fundamental differences between the mode of Corneille and the mode of Racine, in whose plays we meet again that tragic inevitability that we miss in Corneille's.

[1] *Measure for Measure*, II. ii. 161–87 and iv. 1–17.

Shakespeare the Dramatist

Que de soucis flottants, que de confus nuages
Présentent à mes yeux d'inconstantes images!
Douce tranquillité, que je n'ose espérer,
Que ton divin rayon tarde à les éclairer!
Mille agitations, que troubles produisent,
Dans mon coeur ébranlé tour à tour se détruisent:
Aucun espoir n'y coule où j'ose persister;
Aucun effroi n'y règne où j'ose m'arreter.
Mon esprit, embrassant tout ce qu'il s'imagine,
Voit tantôt mon bonheur, et tantôt ma ruine,
Et suit leur vaine idée avec si peu d'effet,
Qu'il ne peut espérer ni craindre tout à fait.

After these twelve lines of lucid and accurate psychological description, she turns to a sixteen-line examination of the problem which has caused her distress. What will happen when Sévère and Polyeucte meet, her affianced lover and her husband? She balances the probabilities as though it were a problem in dynamics, delivering a summary of the case for a quarrel in a way that would do credit to a historian or a psychologist defining a situation to a class. Then she illustrates the conflict decribed in the first twelve lines by changing her assumption and putting, more briefly this time, the considerations that may lead them to forbearance. She returns for another brief period to renew and add to the arguments for the first probability and ends with one line of pious, but obviously unfounded, hope. It is a brilliant speech; a vivid and compact piece of exposition, designed to show us (by what is admittedly a convention) a part of the background to the events of the play. But we cannot rid ourselves of the feeling that it would have carried more conviction in the convention of a messenger's speech. We are not listening to a soul in the grip of its own distracting torment, but to someone narrating another's experience. And it would have served better our understanding of the character and our acceptance of the tragedy if the narrator had not been that character itself. This superb speech is in every line a denial of

Communication in Thought

character, of that hidden correspondence between depth and surface upon which character depends. Whether some effect equivalent to that of drama can be produced by this technique where spirited narrative takes the place of manifold and evocative disclosure is doubtful. What is certain is that Corneille, herein differing essentially from Racine no less than from Shakespeare, attempted to substitute coherent thought throughout his drama for the half incoherent revelation normal to human beings in extremity and in so employing his genius, demonstrated for all time the essentially undramatic nature of demonstration in drama.

With Angelo we move into another world. The two soliloquies form a sequence jumping the significant interval of tormented thinking much as the choice [1] . . .

Note

This chapter was to have been followed by one on 'communication by imagery'. A note in the draft scheme refers to the essay in *The Frontiers of Drama* and a further note reads: 'Communication by imagery, verbal and symbolic (as in Ibsen's S.Ds. etc., Agamemnon's purple carpet) by language, association etc. Lenormand's S.D. for *L'homme et ses fantômes.*' The following extract from 'The Poet's Imagery' (1949) describes the value of the investigation of imagery:

It has given us a knowledge of Shakespeare's habits and processes as a writer. This may act as a corrective to rash assumptions and perhaps play its part in the determining of doubtful cases of authorship, offering evidence complementary to the findings of that bibliographical and textual criticism which revolutionized Shakespeare scholarship at the beginning of this century. But I think its real value will always be rather that of the discipline to which I have just referred. It has taught modern criticism a new awareness of one branch of Shakespeare's technique, and has taught it, by its occasional excesses no less than by its genuine achievement, that no branch of his technique can be studied in isolation or considered

[1] The chapter breaks off in the middle of a sentence. But there is some discussion of one of Angelo's soliloquies, p. 45 above.

without reference to all other aspects of his dramatic art. Its value, that is to say, is aesthetic: it has brought us a step nearer to the understanding of Shakespeare the artist. But as a branch of aesthetics, it will, I think, prove fruitful only in so far as the dramatic function of the images is kept unwaveringly before the critic's mind. The dramatic functions of imagery are many and it would be foolish to suppose that those of us who have discovered some five or six have come to the end of the story. Like the vitamins, they will probably go on revealing themselves until the whole alphabet is needed to label them.

VII

Some Functions of Verbal Music in Drama

THE VERBAL MUSIC OF a play I take to include all that belongs to the sound of its language (as distinguished from the semantic aspect), with its smallest unit the single syllable and its greatest the total effect of the sound in the whole work of art.[1] It is thus an essential aspect of form, which in turn gives significance to content in a work of art; and it offers to the critic a study complementary to that of the language considered as the medium of meaning and of semantic association in the content. But this study on the grand scale constitutes a branch of dramatic aesthetics too vast to enter upon in a brief note, and we need another Coleridge to extend Coleridge's own comments on the function of metre in poetry into the field of the general dramatic function of verbal music.[2] We are all aware of the music on that grand scale, as serving and defining both the content of the play and that underlying apprehension of life from which the play derives. But this awareness must for many of us be intermittent, perhaps vague; and for all but a few it will be limited to a momentary perception that such experience of the music of the play is possible and is in fact one aspect of the play's form and an image of its significance.[3] Yet,

[1] That is what Lascelles Abercrombie calls 'the instrumental form of the poem'. (*Principles of English Prosody* (1923) p. 18, pp. 31–6.)

[2] This is not to belittle the work of recent critics who have discussed specific functions; it is the problem of the 'instrumental form' of the play which is here considered.

[3] 'We are continually conscious of large rhythmic effects which *ought* to combine, if only we had the ability to integrate them, into a single form

125

uncertain as we may be of the nature of this aspect of technique when thus thought of as a whole, we are clear enough about a few of its specific functions. The mere observation in childhood of the transitions from prose to verse in Shakespeare's plays starts the process working and later study brings intimations of the part played by the music in our interpretation perhaps of the mood of a play, perhaps of its form or of the nature of one of its characters. And in this interpretation we may find something complementary to or distinct from that which had been suggested by other aspects of the play and this very divergence may in turn lead to a re-examination, a re-valuation of the other evidence, and so to a reinterpretation of the play, fuller, wiser and taking account of more of those qualifying and modulating implications which are characteristic of Shakespeare and essential to genuine dramatic revelation. As a rule, in these cases, the imagery is found to be at one with the verbal music in conveying this special knowledge to our imaginations; but though music and imagery invariably strengthen and illuminate each other's work, the operation of each is distinct.

Of the specific functions that I have just suggested and of which we are all aware, the most general and all-pervasive is that of transmitting to our imaginations, at a level below the initial revelation and conscious acceptance of character and event, something of the mood or quality of the play.[1] This is clear, at least in its main lines of operation, in many plays. It can be seen in *Macbeth*,[2] where the hurtling pace of the passions

---

corresponding with the whole significance, just as the movement of a sonnet is heard as a whole as well as understood as a whole.' (Abercrombie, op. cit. p. 35.)

[1] This corresponds, of course, with one of the functions of iterative imagery recognized and analysed in detail in the work of Caroline Spurgeon and of Wolfgang Clemen.

[2] The discussion of verbal music, like that of imagery, must obviously be confined to passages which are not textually suspect. This principle, vital for a text such as *Macbeth*, must equally be observed throughout the Canon.

Some Functions of Verbal Music in Drama

and events is conveyed to the imagination primarily perhaps by the systole and diastole of much of the rhythm, by its rapid cadence and suspended pause, and where the contrast between this and certain other, slow-moving rhythms, charged with horror or heaviness of soul, itself serves (amid much else) to contribute to our willing acceptance of the experience of a double, simultaneous tempo.[1] Again, in *Othello*, where there is so much of 'architectural stateliness of quarried speech'[2] as to draw rhythm and cadence into a corresponding stateliness of movement, there is again a significant contrast, in the dissonances frequent in Acts III and IV, which serves to indicate the two planes upon which both the play's events and the characters' experience proceed. The relations of the main musical movements to the prevailing moods or to the structural characteristics in a play may be similarly observed in many others from *Richard II* and *A Midsummer Night's Dream* to *Cymbeline* and *The Winter's Tale*.

But in certain plays that leave a total impression either complex or seemingly confused, it may be that the music (together with the imagery) has a special function, conveying an interpretation of the prevailing mood or a revelation of the underlying apprehension of life which differs from the impression we otherwise receive. In *Troilus and Cressida*, the sustained intensity and tragic passion of the blank verse music are in strong, sometimes in complete contrast with the seeming shapelessness, of plot suggested by the juxtaposition of event, character, and mood.[3] It was this contrast, perhaps as much as any other single factor, which first drew certain critics in this century to

[1] The first of these musical movements is especially clear in passages such as I. iii. 130-42, vii. 1-10; II. ii. 58-64 and the second in III. iv. 122-44; V. v. 9-28. (References are to Craig's edition, O.U.P.)

[2] G. Wilson Knight, 'The *Othello* music'. (*The Wheel of Fire*, ed. 1930, p. 114.)

[3] The function of the verbal music here is inseparable from that of the intense and strongly concentrated imagery.

127

reinterpret this play. And the reinterpretation itself revealed the presence of a profound artistic intention precisely in this contrasting of the functions of different aspects of the technique; in this case, broadly, of the style and of the plotting, the verbal music being a major constituent of that style. The double aspect of the form, with its bewildering and apparently contradictory definitions of content, proved then (as form ever must prove) to be the true definition of that content's deeply conflicting evidence. And it was the verbal music in close relation with the imagery, but conveying its own independent impression, which had qualified the evidence from other aspects of the play and so transformed the total impression of both content and form.

Troilus and Cressida, then, affords evidence of an independent and it may be corrective or modulating function entrusted to the verbal music (or to the music and the imagery) of a play. But we may perhaps go a step further and suggest that this, operating when much else is obscure, has sometimes guided readers to an empirical estimate of the nature of a play's world and of its significance which often proves to have been justified in a reinterpretation of the whole. In, for instance, the notoriously puzzling and much disputed [1] play of *All's Well That Ends Well*, I would suggest that some help in interpretation comes, unexpectedly, from a willing resignation of the imagination to the music of the play's language; something of its nature is thereby disclosed, something even, it may be, of its genesis is hinted at.

The artistic discrepancies of this play, at one level or another, have led some of its critics to the conviction that it is not all Shakespeare's and others to believe it written and re-written at different dates. And yet this play, written admittedly on different levels of imaginative experience and with differing degrees of technical skill, has in its nobler parts or aspects its

[1] So wide are the differences of critical opinion in regard to this play that it is almost impossible to strike a balance between the contradictory views on any important aspect of its art or provenance.

Some Functions of Verbal Music in Drama

own distinctive flavour of quality and sagacity, a flavour which disturbs our first impression with the hint of an artistic intention as yet eluding our imagination. If this be true, is mixed authorship, then, or mixed date, the only possible solution of the conflicting indications of this play? If the intention seems to us obscure, may it not be that it has in fact been obscured, perhaps by some faltering in the process of communication or some incompleteness in the imaginative conception? We have been half-familiarized with this problem, in a slightly different form in *Timon of Athens*; and we know moreover that in the two plays most closely related to *All's Well* we enter the territory of no common experience. Its imagery and its music have, it is true, been condemned for colourless flatness oddly at variance with the style of *Measure for Measure* and still more with that of *Troilus and Cressida*. But in fact the effect, whether of the imagery or of the music of *All's Well* is not wholly negative; certain positive qualities make themselves felt; a quiet if elusive metaphor; a cross-grained piece of syntax that discloses upon examination a complex series of multiple meanings; the music of a seemingly unmemorable line that dwells, surprisingly, in the mind. It is not much. But it is enough to make us suspect that we have two different groups of indications to follow; on the one hand, a recognized defectiveness in plot and characterization, on the other a positive if not wholly successful experiment in the exploration of unfamiliar territories of mind. In fact there is in this play a new and unfamiliar diction and music, one which, though impeded and sometimes silenced by the overruling causes we have already suggested, nevertheless persists sometimes to the verge of achievement and always with consistency:

> The fated skye
> Giues vs free scope, onely doth backward pull
> Our slow designes, when we our selues are dull.[1]

[1] *All's Well*, I. i. 236–8.

Shakespeare the Dramatist

Here, almost alone in Shakespeare's plays, we are in a world where the words do not 'sing and shine'; their music is that of low-toned, meditative speech, where no splendour or sudden glory of image evokes in response a memorable or poignant cadence. The lines move softly, almost silently onward; we follow, intent upon an elusive meaning which may gradually fade even while holding the promise of a growing lucidity; there is seldom, except perhaps in some of Helena's early speeches, full release from the need for this intent and absorbed observation. We are not borne onward, as in *Measure for Measure* (and still more in *Troilus and Cressida*) upon succeeding waves of rhythm; we move, as though upon a broad, slow, faintly luminous flood, towards an undefined shore. Sound and imagery alike seem to explore a difficult borderland of vision, evoking in us the expectation of a distinctive, but unfamiliar experience.

> For we are old, and on our quick'st decrees
> Th'inaudible, and noiselesse foot of time
> Steales, ere we can effect them.[1]

These are the cadences that dwell in the mind, and their burden is of slowness and weight. They are, moreover, dramatic, not undramatic, germane to the characters, the expression of their meditative and reflective minds, and alien to those of stirring, fierce or passionate spirits. One hesitates, therefore, to accept such music as an accident in an otherwise banal and unoriginal play; rather, it seems the expression of a hidden element in the play, perhaps the index of an attempt to image an experience that at all other points escaped.

If then the language and music are what they are because of something that they have to express, may we not, bearing in mind the function of verbal music in other plays, submit ourselves to its guidance here, letting it lead us, if it will, to the core of the play's nature? We have described the music and

[1] *All's Well*, V. iii. 40–2.

Some Functions of Verbal Music in Drama

language of this play as indices of the movements of still and meditative minds and the syntax can point us to a corresponding world of thought, to thought needing the utmost precision for its quiet but unfamiliar explorations and, even so, often eluding capture. And so we meet the significant paradox of this play, considered as a piece of dramatic art, that it contains thoughtful but not passionate characters and speech and nothing to bring about tragic conflict or tumultuous action whether tragic or comic. But what has drama to do with so passionless a play? (For passionless it indeed is, and it is I think one of the functions of the verbal music to guide us to this perception.) When Shakespeare came to write the four plays that closed his career, he had solved that question. Another sphere of experience had taken precedence of the passions and they were subdued, held in the background of the scene, so that we watch them through a haze that dims their brilliance to opalescence while listening meanwhile to other intimations. And, moreover, it is in these last plays that we meet, firm and clear, the cadences that have haunted us in the distances of *All's Well*. For in this earlier play he appears to attempt the revelation of a world like that of *Cymbeline* and *The Winter's Tale* where the chief characters, whether young or old, possess a ripe nobility, because high bearing in them is illuminated with courtesy and with urbane forbearance, and because chivalry has disciplined the boisterous force of the passions, turning them into channels graved by purpose and dedicating them to its intent. It may be that when *All's Well* was written, the time for this attempt had not yet come; but it may nevertheless be that we are right in following the indication given by the verbal imagery and believing that some such attempt, even if imperfectly achieved was then made. If this is true, then the function of the music has indeed been of some significance in determining the total effect of the play upon our imaginations; the function (shared only by the imagery) of disclosing something of the poet's intention which was else invisible. Now, we often find that the verbal music has a function analogous to this, but illuminating not so much the mood or hidden intention of the play as a part of the content itself. We have already noticed that it may confirm or corroborate our impression of the nature of a play's structure and it is a commonplace of criticism that it is responsible for a large part of our understanding of certain characters and moods, strengthening thus the evidence of the rest of the play. But it is possible for verbal music to give us hints of a different kind, impressions of character at variance from those made by the other evidence and insisting upon a reconsideration of the bearings of this and in the end upon a reinterpretation of the whole. It may thus operate upon our understanding of character in a way closely akin to that which we attempted to trace when following its guidance in our interpretation of a special aspect of the play of *All's Well*, conveying an idea in seeming contradiction to the other indications in the play that nevertheless proves indispensable to a right reading of those others.

It is sometimes worth while to make a running survey of the speeches of certain characters, pretending, for the moment, that the music is our only clue to character, for we may find that it does indeed sometimes offer clues of the kind we have just suggested. The changes of mood and bearing in the character, for instance, of Coriolanus receive some curious illuminations from this treatment.[1]

The first phase of Coriolanus's speech-music reveals certain aspects of his character that are simultaneously confirmed by a multitude of indications and a cloud of witness. In the rhythm of his first speeches,[2] all is alert and crisp; brief sections abruptly

---

[1] It must be plainly admitted that there is an almost symbiotic relation between verbal music and imagery in the speech of Coriolanus. But the two are nevertheless individuals; their functions in the life partnership can be distinguished though they are hardly ever (or only momentarily) at variance in their purposes.

[2] I. i. 173–94, 196–206, 234–57.

Some Functions of Verbal Music in Drama

alternate with longer passages that are rapid but shapely; when his language becomes colloquial it remains rhythmical and when he is angry the rhythm takes on a swift, lilting movement like quick waves. His long speeches are thus complete and rounded, if simple, musical studies. The memory of this remains with us, so that when we meet him next in the battle-scenes[1] we observe that even anger, which breaks up his syntax but not his rhythms,[2] leaves the impression of speed without hurry, of the leaping energy of a fiery spirit finding its natural music and secure in itself. This is, I think, of great importance, for, with the exception of his last great speech in the forum, I doubt whether Coriolanus is ever again in absolute harmony with his own deeds until the end. And I doubt, further, whether we should altogether realize how strong is that harmony here, were it not that the movement of the verse, which never stumbles, conveys to us at unawares this sense of the sure-footedness of his spirit in such surroundings.

Back in Rome, he still speaks the music of the opening scenes, but now with some modifications. An irritable movement sets in when he strives against Cominius's praises[3] and there is, as always, an interesting change of music when he speaks to Virgilia,[4] when the cadences become melodious if simple, the speed and force of movement cease and the rhythms become clear and calm.[5] The Coriolanus of the second act begs his votes in prose and so the characteristic music momentarily disappears. But, when he is alone for a few moments, he, like the senators of *Othello*, chooses rhyme for his 'sentences' and converses with himself in a slow, sardonic movement that should warn us against accepting as final the earlier limitations whether of music or of character. In his contest with the tribunes in the third act,[6] the familiar, strong rhythms

[1] I. iv–viii.   [2] I. iv. 30–42.   [3] I. ix. 13–19.   [4] II. i. 196–8.
[5] This special music evoked by Virgilia recurs in Coriolanus's speech whenever he meets her.
[6] III. i. 25 seq.

return; harder, but not so buoyant; graver, but no less powerful. When rage quickens them, they have the pace of the
earliest speeches and the hardness of this new mood; there are
long verse paragraphs[1] (whose content is tough, hard thought,
as well as passion), and these are swift, but not now abrupt.
This is his finest and strongest music and the current of it is
rapid and deep. Finally the climax,[2] the accents come like the
strokes of a hammer, driven home by alliteration and the
sounds of hard, splitting consonants. Yet there is measure and
control in every prosodic phrase and in its relation to others
and to the verse paragraph which is now the prosodic unit.

Although the last lines of this scene (III. iii) have thus a
sound unlike any we have met before,[3] it is with some shock
that we realize in the fourth act that part of their movement
has become habitual to a character which, in the final stages of
that conflict and in the interval since, has entered upon a new
phase, suddenly and deliberately changing its outward form.
The music of the next three scenes is still measured, grave,
and controlled; a solemn music and more nearly conventional
although the cadences grow colourless and there is less of that
individual syncopation that came of the hurry and precipitation
of syllables in the outbursts of wrath.[4]

The same measured, almost stately movement continues
through the rest of the act, commonplace in music as in the
sentiment that the music accompanies, sometimes with a high
proportion of regular lines[5] in sharp contrast to the rhythms of

[1] III. i. 63–73, 90–111, 118–38, 139–60.   [2] III. iii. 118–33.

[3] Though they have in part been anticipated, as we later realize in movements in II. iii and III. i, notably at II. iii. 120–30.

[4] The pace quickens and some of the old movement returns momentarily
to accompany the image of the lonely dragon (IV. i. 29–31). This too recurs
in the final acts.

[5] In one short passage (IV. iv. 12–24), four lines are without variation and
several others only slightly modified from the norm. This is quite unlike
Coriolanus's earlier rhythms and its smoothness here is ominous.

Some Functions of Verbal Music in Drama

Act I, sometimes in sustained verse paragraphs with long prosodic units from which the elasticity of the earlier leaping movement has vanished. Yet the verse has taken on a firm and steady tread, the image of a mood which seems compact of control and vigilance, where only a phrase or two[1] remains to disturb our assurance. In his long speech to Aufidius,[2] we meet this new Coriolanus, a man seemingly controlled and wholly integrated, the music of whose speech contrasts as clearly with the fiery, athletic movement of his earlier verse as it does with the plain straightforward prose of North upon which it rests.[3] By the end of this scene, after which we do not see Coriolanus again until the final movement begins in Act V, the music of his speech has so grown in solidity and consistency that it almost drowns our doubts and bewilderments. This music is maintained, with certain modifications natural to the formality of the situation, through Act V, scene ii.

But early in the third scene of the fifth act a third phase is disclosed, a music which gradually overpowers the colourless, prosaic movement of the opening of the scene and, after some twenty lines, begins to break it up: a touch of a more vivid movement (ll. 24–6) picks up those scattered phrases which, with diminishing frequency, had recalled the rhythms prompted by the image of the dragon in his fen; for two lines

---

[1] As in the lines (84–9) in the middle of the otherwise deliberate speech to Aufidius in IV. v.

[2] IV. v. 71–107.

[3] In this speech, in which the quantity and weight of the rhythm reveal the new Coriolanus, there are groups of lines (71–3, 77–9) in which the verbal music is the only substantial difference between North's prose and Shakespeare's verse; an unimportant word drops out, the position of another shifts, and the movement is completely changed, while leaving the content of the verse almost identical with that of the prose. In these, and a few passages which approach them in closeness to the source, we find the rhythm momentarily responsible for the differences in our impressions of North's and of Shakespeare's characters.

(ll. 27–8) we hear again the music that from the beginning has been associated with Virgilia; after a brief assertion of control (ll. 29–33) a hurried, irregular, excited movement breaks in (ll. 33–6) recalling, though with certain differences, the rhythms of the early acts. This is a prosodically surprising passage. In less than twenty lines we have listened to four different and by now familiar kinds of music, three of which had been excluded with increasing rigour since towards the end of the third act. We have heard, that is, a significant piece of musical inter-pretation, perhaps the clearest intimation given us at this point [1] that buried passions are not dead, that they are battling for their rights against the metallic smoothness of demeanour imposed by Coriolanus's new impersonation and that their outbreak, like that of all suppressed and maltreated passion, may take unexpected courses and end in havoc. For much of the rest of the scene, these four movements will be found to contend with each other, but the rising excitement hinted at in the movement of ll. 35–6 begins (ll. 56–62) to dominate the rest. Its rhythms are blunt and commonplace, sometimes crude and theatrical, and sometimes deliberately repetitive in stress and cadence; suggesting the monotonous emphasis of an in-experienced speaker, italicising sounds at regular intervals to carry conviction and to seem convinced. This is the perfect musical image of hysteria, of blind emotion fighting against blind control. After some lines of formal speech again and Volumnia's long speeches, the climax of this music of hysteria returns (ll. 183–93), its repetitions, the heavy, lurching move-ment of the lines, the loss of elasticity in the relations between stresses and vocalic quality, all revealing the false and theatrical emotion which finds its natural expression upon the imagistic plane in the recurrent picture of the actor. After this the formal movement returns, but now without the artificiality of the corresponding passages in Act IV and the beginning of Act V, and we never hear again any of the music peculiar to Corio-

[1] Except, again, for that of the imagery.

lanus until a brief outbreak of the first phase (V. v. 129–31) closes the play.

The third scene of the fifth act, then, has made clear one of the dramatic functions of verbal music, it reveals faithfully the insecurity of the temporary integration of Coriolanus's character, the artificiality of his rigid self-command, the hysterical movement of false emotion in conflict with this false reserve and the return of his mind on to its balance again at the end, and this it does in terms of those musical movements that we have learnt to associate with certain of his emotions or states of mind throughout the play. The sound, that is to say, here images a hidden condition of mind which is indicated by no other means except the imagery. Moreover, that same agency has warned us in the early part of the play, by the peculiar music associated with Virgilia, that there may be such hidden depths and in these middle acts by the recurrence of the dragon's music[1] that the problem of the injury done to those hidden depths of his nature is not to be solved by increasing the pressure of a blind control or by the deliberate impersonation of a man of iron.

But when we have once heard these indications we can no longer close our ears to them and the surface facts of Coriolanus's character and bearing now become of interest chiefly in terms of their contradiction to an unknown, hidden self. Once we have accepted the presence of that other self known to no other character except Virgilia – who is, as we remember, 'silence' – we read all other evidences with fresh eyes and may discover in Coriolanus, hidden, undeveloped, unexpressed and unrecognized, above all, to himself, a poet who delighted in the icicle 'that's curded by the frost from purest snow', a poet for whom the war's great business was his only image of glory, but whose mind at its most bewildered never forgot the nature of integrity nor, in its most seemingly triumphant impersonation,

---

[1] See above (note 4, p. 134).

forgave to itself the crime of compromising with its own inward truth.

This necessarily brief sketch has omitted much corroborative detail and left much of the field unexplored. But I hope I have made clear the suggestion that in certain places the submitting of our imaginations to the impression given by the verbal music may offer us a clue to interpretation, whether of character or of structure, that is not to be had elsewhere. Because of what I may call the symbiotic relationship of imagery and verbal music in drama, such revelation is I believe generally potential in the imagery also. But the functions of the two are, as I have said, distinct, and, in order to let this appear, I have deliberately separated them in making these suggestions so that the part played by the music alone could be the clearer.

Note

This chapter was to have been followed by a conclusion to this section of the book, 'gathering up findings from specimens analysed and generalizing from them (making it clear throughout that they were only specimens, by grouping the mass of references here). Perhaps some grouping of dramatists in order:

i. Mainly expository. Seldom dramatic throughout.
ii. Mingled, the majority of minors (*a*) limitedly dramatic throughout, (*b*) intermittently dramatic.
iii. Essentially evocative and so essentially dramatic. Only Shakespeare in his maturity gives us a world *wholly* of secret impressions. And so gives us the secret and hidden world.'

VIII

Shakespeare and Ibsen as Dramatic Artists

A S THE WORLD COMES to understand better something of the greatness of Ibsen as a dramatic artist, we realize that his art stands by itself, not only, as does that of every great poet, by the impress of his individuality, but because he attempts in drama something which is without precise counterpart in the work of the major dramatists who are his peers. Aeschylus, Sophocles, Euripides, and Shakespeare are all poetic dramatists and their art is not only expressed but conceived in terms of poetry; the language of poetry, charged with imagery, and the verbal music which is a part of their verse are both integral to their conception and inseparable from the form of the whole play. But Ibsen during much of his career wrote prose and the dramatic mode of some of his noblest plays is determined by or dictates the prose vehicle, just as theirs were determined by or dictated the vehicle of poetry. He chose, that is to say, the mode which is associated primarily with statement, with description, with argument, with philosophical thought; not that which is associated with poetic experience. He chose to be what we may perhaps call a philosopher-dramatist.

Now here is something of a paradox, for the nature of drama seems, so far as we can judge, to demand a complete concealment of the artist's self, his beliefs, and his ideas, a loss of his personality in those of the people he creates; while they may have thoughts and opinions, may criticize and interpret the world in which he presents them, he must not. His function is to create an image of a world, not to describe, explain, or

139

analyse it. And this function determines the mode of his writing also, for, just as the nature of drama forbids the dramatist to state his own interpretation of man's life or destiny, so does it also forbid him to describe his characters or cause them, except in special cases, to describe themselves. The other four great dramatists whom we have named his peers lead us into understanding of characters and events by awakening in us a profound imaginative sympathy with these characters and these events; so profound that often we cannot express in words what we have apprehended in the depths of our minds. We learn from these plays as we do from life, at half-unawares, by unrecorded impressions and by knowledge hidden from our conscious thought. For they are in truth an image of life and not a sermon, however noble, upon life's issues. That wise critic, Maurice Morgann, said, nearly two hundred years ago, that Shakespeare had 'contrived to make secret impressions upon us', and the longer we study the work of Shakespeare the more deeply are we convinced that it is by these secret impressions that we guide ourselves in our interpretation of his plays.

Here then is a contrast, seemingly fundamental, between the poetic, evocative mode of Shakespeare and the way in which Ibsen, in certain of the plays written after 1875, presents for our consideration problems whose nature he defines for us and whose importance he illuminates simultaneously by debates between characters and selection and juxtaposition of episodes which themselves approximate to argument. And so, at the end of a careful study of, say, *Pillars of the Community*, we know or ought to know something of what Ibsen thought about truth and lies in public life and those of us who have studied his work through many years find it comparatively easy to agree upon his reading of life and upon his scale of values. At least we know that truth, in public and private life, truth in the heart, was a thing he valued so highly that he testified to its virtue directly or indirectly in nearly every play he wrote and that, close to it and inseparably associated with it in his work, we find certain other great values: freedom, love, responsibility. But no man has yet been able to say what Shakespeare thought of life, though many have tried and by many roads. All we can certainly say is that whatever we know he knew before us; that he is the eternal companion of our experience. And that means that for each of us he is something different.

Now here we have clearly a sundering difference between Shakespeare and Ibsen in their initial conception of their art, in that vision of a portion of life which constitutes the inspiration of a play. And we shall not be surprised then to find that Shakespeare reveals a character, say that of Ophelia, by means of hints that cannot be understood until we bring to bear upon them the witness of the whole play and that he does something very like that with the widely different character of, for instance, Coriolanus. These are both unable to express their underlying selves in speech and action, the one because she is emotionally inarticulate, the other, though eloquent, because he so profoundly misunderstands himself that we only discover his hidden nature by the aid of Shakespeare's 'secret impressions'. Utterly unlike this is Ibsen's way with the character of, say, Karsten Bernick, whose self-knowledge is so nearly complete that he only with great difficulty shuts his eyes to the inference that follows from it. When once he has been forced to acknowledge this, he proves the extent of his self-knowledge by an analysis as lucid as a philosopher's. Utterly unlike Shakespeare's mode, but again illustrative of his own, is that of a host of other thoughtful men and women in Ibsen's plays who have won self-knowledge at the conscious, intellectual level and are themselves our guides in the interpretation of their lives: Nora Helmer, Mrs Alving, Halvard Solness. They are all, in a wide sense of the term, philosophers, just as is their creator.

And in the same way we may contrast the seemingly loose, evocative technique of Shakespeare's structure in *Macbeth* with

Shakespeare the Dramatist

that of Ibsen in *Pillars of the Community, A Doll's House, An Enemy of the People, The Wild Duck, Hedda Gabler*. In *Macbeth* we are carried forward by great leaps of the imagination from event to event, their psychological significance determining Shakespeare's instinctive selection and their evocative power such that we too pass from one to the other with instinctive understanding of their hidden relation and their inevitable result. In clear contrast stands the exquisite articulation of Ibsen's plotting, which demonstrates, with compelling logic, the inevitable path of cause and consequence.

All this is clear enough and has so long been recognized that I do not propose to dwell upon it, but rather, if I may, to attempt to correct the balance of some of our assumptions. For I think, and I speak now chiefly of English criticism and of the conclusions accepted by lovers of Ibsen in my own country, that we at one time laid undue emphasis on this particular group of his plays and that this still results in an interpretation of Ibsen which tends to look too steadily at the philosopher in him and too seldom at the poet. I should like to suggest that we may find in Ibsen too the evocative mode of the great poetic dramatist, and that, not merely where, as in *Peer Gynt*, we cannot fail to see it, but also in those very prose plays where we have taken too little thought of it. The task of writing what is virtually poetic drama in the mood and manner of prose was one of such difficulty that we may, without disrespect, say that Ibsen did not at once achieve it. That he did achieve it, and in somewhat the same terms as Shakespeare, and that we can perhaps indicate some stages in his progress towards it, is the suggestion that I should like to make.

I will not stay now to substantiate what I have said of the group of prose plays that begin with *Pillars of the Community*, but will ask for a measure of agreement when I say that in the greater part of most of them we find a dramatist who differs widely from Sophocles and Shakespeare, one whose method is essentially demonstrative, whose major characters are often

Shakespeare and Ibsen as Dramatic Artists

self-explanatory and whose structure is often itself an argument as cogent as a logical *catena*.[1] Nevertheless, even in these plays, the two modes can be found side by side, hints of this duality being discernible as early as *Pillars of the Community*. But at the height of his power, in the final group of plays, evocation and not demonstration controls both the revelation of character and the unfolding of event that constitutes plot. We find in *Ghosts* a clear instance of the double process and in *Rosmersholm* a supreme revelation of evocative technique in prose drama.

We shall agree, I think, in saying that the structure of *Ghosts* is one of the most beautiful pieces of formal art to be found in drama. Perhaps the most interesting aspect of this structure is to be found in the grouping of the characters, which in turn determines the logic of event. Some critics nowadays like to call this the spatial aspect of a play; it may be thought of as a picture and, if we adopt Lessing's convenient distinction, as static in time and extended in space. In studying it we consider the characters not primarily in terms of their experience, but in terms of the illumination we receive from their juxtaposition and their relative positions in the composition. Looked at like this, *Ghosts* may be seen as a simple, but massive group of statuary, in which the characters balance each other in respect of the central theme or thought, to the definition of which they all contribute; the five are so selected that each brings to the central idea of the play one part of the final, composite effect. The dead hand of convention and duty has subdued to its purposes Pastor Manders, who has thus become its vehicle and its exponent, but it has driven Mrs Alving to rebellion and so to emancipation of thought. Modifying the contrasted positions of these two, are three others who show the workings

[1] This is not, of course, to confuse Ibsen's technique or mode with that in which the characters are the mouthpieces, not of their own knowledge but of the dramatist's, and where the movement of the plot is less that of cogent argument than of the punctual revolutions of a machine.

of that same compulsion upon related, yet differing, minds and characters. Each of these three provides a variation on the theme and in representative proportions: Regine has rebelled without thought or heart-searching and has suffered the degeneration that comes of rejecting the good and the bad alike in a given social code; her 'father', Engstrand, as immoral as she but more shrewd, has cunningly observed the workings of the system and found his account in playing upon its victims; Osvald has escaped psychological harm only to be destroyed by the physical consequences from which nothing could save him. Each of the five bears direct or indirect testimony to the weight of this dead hand and their relationship demonstrates the operation of the curse; a Laokoon group of figures still imprisoned or too late emancipated to maintain valid life.

With this image of the play in mind, we can observe Ibsen's method in more detail. In the first place, each character is so related to the theme of his play that whichever one we study we still have in view those others whose functions are complementary to its function, who depend upon it for their balance as it depends on them for its. And, in the second, the structure of the whole, with its living tension, is itself an argument, a demonstration of the tragic effects of the suppression of truth and freedom in the characters and fates of this compact and closely welded group of figures.

Ibsen, as we have said, begins his groupings with the figures of Manders and Mrs Alving, in frank though not at first unfriendly opposition at the centre of the play: Manders, a man moulded by slavery to convention and totally unaware of the evil of this, since for him the laws of custom have taken the place of honest thought and opinion, a man readily persuaded that evil is good and good evil, provided only that the conventions of his time and place give their assent: Mrs Alving, a woman who has outgrown false standards as completely as Manders has accepted them, who has discarded the sentimentality and insincerity in which both he and she had been reared and has learned through bitterness and self-discipline to speak the truth in her heart; who has developed to the point at which she can understand and repudiate shams and deceits, whether in Manders or in a society which is solidly against her. His distinction thus made manifest, his two central positions thus defined, Ibsen proceeds with strength and economy to support them by the other three – we might almost say by the other four – characters; Osvald, who has lived in and experienced the healthy world in which work and living are joyous things and has recognized its normality without going through a mental crisis to win that recognition; Regine, his half-sister, who has similar instincts, made crude, coarse, and rebellious in part by her own heritage, but in part also by her life in a society which condemns and shrinks from them; Engstrand, the embodiment of servility and cunning fostered by falsehoods, traditions, and lies. Finally, there is the spirit of the dead Captain Alving, who can hardly in fairness be left out of the character list. At the beginning of the play, something of a mystery, his relation to the central theme is undefined, but his character and conduct receive three different interpretations before we uncover the original man and with that final uncovering the last touch is put to the tragic argument implicit in the structure of this Laokoon group.

So much for the spatial aspect of this play. If this image has served to illuminate in any degree the cogency of the structure, the way in which Ibsen has made of the very juxtaposition of these characters an argument upon the central theme, it has served its purpose. But the temporal aspect of the structure, the movement of events through time (the other half of Lessing's convenient distinction), this again offers an elucidation of the idea Ibsen is concerned to convey. The nature of 'duty' dictated by the dead hand of the past is gradually illuminated by the emergence of an alternative conception of man's destiny as the theme of joy is gradually defined by those charged with the attack upon the 'ghosts' of conventions and lies. The forward movement of the action is inevitable, with the inevitableness of that which is perfectly natural. Mrs Alving and Manders have known each other for a quarter of a century; we recognize from the first that they have a store of memories which they now call up and now evade. It is therefore natural that they should discuss their past and inevitable that discussion should end explosively, with wreck and ruin and revelation that disclose the past and precipitate the future; the logic is flawless that drives us step by step to the conclusion. Here again, in the movement of event no less than in the essential opposition of the figures, it is character that serves the theme. Thus the great scenes in which Mrs Alving and Pastor Manders interpret to themselves and to us the central idea and the meaning of the action have many simultaneous functions, illuminating the past, so that we see it reaching forward to strangle the present, revealing first Manders's then Mrs Alving's interpretation of all that had happened in the recent history of the fated house of Alving, stripping away the deception, exposing his self-deception. It brings into clear and implacable contrast the two interpretations of life, of the relation of the individual to society and even more of the true organization of society itself. Moreover, it does this with the intensity that grows out of tragic passion and the memory of passion – just how much, we gradually discover as the play goes on – and it has the con-centration of a dramatic crisis combined with the lucidity of Ibsen's conversational analyses in *Pillars of the Community* and in *A Doll's House*. This can only be done by setting the events far enough in the past for thought to have matured and cleared for Mrs Alving and hardened and petrified for Manders, so that the characters speak with absolute certainty of their mean-ing, the passion stirring and deepening their thought but not confusing it.

But is there perhaps something that we have passed by in describing the compulsive logic of the character-grouping and of the ordered sequence of events? In describing, that is, the

Shakespeare and Ibsen as Dramatic Artists

demonstrative and argumentative functions of the structure of this play, those aspects of its form that mark it as the work of a philosopher-dramatist? I think there is and that we shall find in Ibsen's treatment of one character and in part of his treatment of another something that we first apprehend by the aid of intimations closely akin to the 'secret impressions' of the mode of evocative drama. To put it paradoxically, there are six additional characters in this play, all of whom are revealed by technique more profoundly evocative than that of the later Jean Jacques Bernard and the *Théâtre de Silence*. In studying the revelation of these characters we find ourselves in the presence of the dramatist who was later, in *Rosmersholm*, to create a great part of his play out of hints, silences, and intimations.

Mrs Alving changes in the course of the play. At the beginning, we might expect her to be a static character, one who had made terms finally with life and would maintain her position to the end. But, and this is one of the triumphs of Ibsen's art, when the explosions and upheavals of the second and third acts shatter her world, she responds to them not by a hardening rigidity, but by further exploration and discovery. The principle of growth is still at work in her; she is a living spirit still. We watch her evolve under our eyes from the clear-sighted, unsentimental woman we first met into one who can see not merely that 'duty' has poisoned her life, sacrificed her to a lie and starved her of reality, but that she herself has contributed to her own tragedy. Reared in terms of duty and obligation, she in her turn had starved the joy of life in another person, in the husband whom nature had endowed with that joy. She recognizes this and admits it, making thereby a great stride forward into a larger freedom. Not for her to go through the remainder of her life, like the tragic figure of Mrs Solness, reiterating miserably the phrase 'It was only my duty'. In this moment she comes within measurable distance of recognizing another 'duty', to joy, to gladness, and to love, a duty akin to Wordsworth's 'Stern daughter of the voice of God' of whom nevertheless he could also say 'Nor know we anything so fair As is the smile upon thy face'.

But this discovery makes us pause, precisely as certain discoveries about Ophelia or Coriolanus make us pause, to reconsider in its light something we had perhaps passed over. The principle of growth is still alive in her. Then the principle of growth must have been in her from the beginning and there must be a longer history of its working than that contained in the events of the play. When we see that, we see suddenly that Ibsen has revealed to us not two phases of Mrs Alving's spiritual growth but five, all of them necessary to our understanding of her but three of them belonging to the distant past of the play and evoked by touches, by hints, by implications. Long ago there had been a credulous and romantic girl, the untrained, uneducated child of a sterile upper-class society, who committed her first deadly sin by making a marriage that betrayed her own instincts and desires. (For Ibsen, here as always, this crime must be expiated by repentance and tears.) This is the first Mrs Alving, the woman who, coerced by those set in authority over her, had married a rich man whom she did not love instead of the poor pastor whom she did. The next, I fancy, is the woman who, recoiling from the vices she had helped to drive him to, left her husband, only to be shepherded back into the path of 'duty'. Into the path of duty, and by Manders, but not into the path of love by her own will. From this there slowly evolved the strong, hard, dominating woman, the 'femme maîtrise', who set herself to save the family name for her son by thrusting this husband still further out of her life, putting all the force of her will to building for him a false reputation of nobility. From this in turn evolved the woman, clear-sighted but still unpitying, whom we meet at the beginning of the play. In the third phase we catch glimpses of a dangerous likeness to Gunhild Borkman, but her love for her son, unlike Gunhild's, had been selfless and unpossessive and through it she was suffered to work out her

Shakespeare and Ibsen as Dramatic Artists

salvation. Five characters, instead of one. These are the things that enrich a play and enrich it with the infinite extensions of the poetic imagination.

But Ibsen the evocative poet has not done with us yet. He has still in reserve Captain Alving – one had better say at once three Captain Alvings. The dead captain cannot appear in the play; but his ghost is one of the most powerful of those that walk. Beside his continual half-seen presence, the paradoxical absent figures of the *Théâtre de Silence* become dim shadows. We discover him in reverse as we discover much in *Rosmersholm*, beginning with the nearest appearance and guided gradually to hints of the earlier and of the underlying reality. First comes the good citizen, the man of philanthropic activities that Manders and general opinion recognize, the man to whose noble life and services the memorial is to be unveiled. Then follows the drunken, worn-out rake that Mrs Alving shows us – the man who had only been kept from disgracing his name by being hidden in the background, while his wife built up the fiction of his noble philanthropic activities by doing the work herself. And finally we discover the man that she, illuminated by his own son Osvald, sees for the first time at the end, a man whose love of life had been poisoned, thwarted, and debased by living in a society which saw nothing but evil in that joy.

If we perceive this in *Ghosts*, we are I think prepared to recognize here a play which has two strains, the philosopher-dramatist designing the great argument of the central theme and dedicating to its demonstration the character-grouping and progressive definition of the ideas and the poet-dramatist so widening the implications of his characters' experience that we find ourselves in the presence of poetic drama, of the creative and evocative mode.

Now it is my belief that in the later plays, especially in those from *The Wild Duck* onwards, this latter mode gradually prevails over the first; that the poet of *Peer Gynt* slowly resumes the mastery over philosopher, social critic, and satirist. Nothing could alter the fact that Ibsen had written the prose plays, just as nothing in Milton's later poetic career could wipe out the effects of his long digression into prose-writing between *Comus* and *Paradise Lost*. A 'born poet' does now and then fall 'upon an age of prose'; not an age in which poetry is not written, but an age in which it is not lived, an age, that is, in which the matter of men's experience, the habit of their thought and the language they exchange seem all to be prosaic, argumentative, or matter-of-fact. In such an age, the drama, mirroring its mood, will tend to divide upon this very issue, associating romantic subject with poetic vehicle and the interpretation of familiar life with the prose vehicle and the prosaic mood. Nevertheless, the mood of that age must enter the poet's mind as a part of his experience and, if he continues to write, it will partly determine the form of his communication. No other way, no other course of development, is possible for him, for, by the nature of his function, he cannot either exclude experience or set deliberate limits to the process of communication. But what the great poet may yet do is to transmute the experience he must not reject, the forms he must necessarily use and so, ultimately, the age itself, into the prose of whose life and thought he had fallen. There greets us at this point one of those paradoxes that illuminate the way of the artist; for the life that, as an artist, he had seemed to lose, is then restored to him, a greater life than he could have reached without the assimilation and transmutation of the obstinate, intransigent, alien prose of the world. It is a commonplace of criticism to say that without the religious and political tracts on which Milton spent his middle years, there would have been no Conclave in Hell. It is equally certain that without the long preoccupation with moral issues, practical, and at least in part critical and philosophical, Ibsen would not have emerged where he did in *The Wild Duck*. In the interval since *The Pretenders* (and even in that play the process was already beginning) he has taken into his imagination the moral habit of his age, its preoccupation, genuine or hypocritical, with issues that are in essence social and ethical, as Milton assimilated political and religious controversy. And because he is of major stature, he too at length transmutes the experience into a War in Heaven, creating a mode of communication in which the mental habits of the men of his time can find full expression, in drama which can reach the grand scale of poetry precisely because it has neither denied them nor obeyed them. He has made a new art, a new kind of drama, because instead of accepting as his material the interpretation his contemporaries made of themselves and as his mode the habit of their thinking, he has subdued them and it, transferring their warfare from counting-houses and stove-heated villas to the plains of eternity. And this done, he too, like Milton, fulfilled also the third condition, for he transmuted in turn the habit and the thinking of that age which had threatened to subdue him, bringing back to Europe a drama urgent and alive, reaching the minds of men as only a living drama could still reach them.

Now Shakespeare's way was different, since his age and his men were predominantly neither moral, political nor religious but human and explorers of human life. But the ends of the two dramatists are alike, for they converge in poetry, which is the destiny of drama. Ibsen could not have followed the poetic mode continuously through his middle phases, for to have done so would have been to reject the material immediately about him, that habit of life which he must work in and work upon if his art were to reach the common roots of that and of all other ways of life. But precisely because of this his last plays fulfil, in terms of his own world, the destiny of drama; they are prophetic and creative because, beneath their seemingly prosaic demeanour, they are poetic and evocative. He found European drama at its best accomplished, critical, observant, and entertaining; he left it restored to its ancient mastery of men's souls.

Now the final phase of this is to be seen in the late plays. But, as I have suggested, the process by which it was achieved may in part be guessed at when we look at those of an earlier date in which Ibsen 'fell', in a sense not strictly implicit in Matthew Arnold's, upon his 'age of prose'. I have confined my hints in speaking of *Ghosts* to purely technical questions and to a special aspect of technique, that of the mode of writing. There is not time for more (nor time indeed for this in any proper fullness) but I am convinced that what we may there see in a single aspect of his craft represents something that is characteristic also of the whole field of his content, the shaping of his material, the underlying thought, and his apprehension of life. And if we now turn to the later plays it will be again to look at this aspect of the technique, leaving it, as before, to represent in miniature the poet's mind.

Ibsen works still, in this later phase, in terms of the habits of thought that the men of his age imposed upon themselves, but the prosaic demeanour, the argumentative or philosophical elucidation, belongs now to his characters alone and no longer in part to their creator. His way now is to reveal to us by hints and suggestions a hidden self at variance with the surface, a self unknown to or unacknowledged by the conscious, active mind of the character. Here is again the poetic and evocative mode that we saw in *Ghosts*; our imaginations act upon these hints to reinterpret the characters' judgements of themselves and of each other. The conversation of Hedda Gabler, focused though it is upon her tastes, her views, her opinions, tells us hardly anything of her inner experience, so that there have been readers whom her suicide has taken by surprise. But this smooth mask, the smoother for seeming to declare itself openly, is momentarily broken by instants of self-revelation (the threat to burn off Thea's hair, the actual burning of her 'child'), which, because of the sudden glimpse of molten passion at work beneath, reveal at once the danger, the significance, and the tragedy of the mask. To work thus, to contradict by a single touch the evidence that a character has

Shakespeare and Ibsen as Dramatic Artists

painfully built up throughout the play, is to work in the way of Shakespeare with Ophelia or Coriolanus; it is the technique of evocation, not of statement. In the same way we are led to divine the past deeds and experiences of characters, not by their own elucidation of them, but by their fumbling approaches to self-discovery or by those touches of contradiction which re-interpret an apparently self-evident picture. Thea, Ellida, Solness, Ella Rentheim, and Gunhild Borkman, all in their different ways lay trembling or uncertain hands upon clues that lead them back through their past to an understanding that we discover with them and, like them, imperfectly. General Gabler, though less often spoken of, is closer to our elbow even than Captain Alving. The incidents in *Rosmersholm* fall half fortuitously, more nearly as do the events of *Macbeth*; they either have no logical inevitability, or if they have, that is not what we notice; in themselves they are nothing, their function is to provoke continuing reflection in us and in the characters. In *Little Eyolf* it is the slender hints, the almost invisible references, that reveal the strength of the compulsions determining the relationship of the four central characters, and stifling in different ways the life of each. In *John Gabriel Borkman* the in-driven natures of the older people lead them to talk at length and without social prevarication about their past tragedies and their schemes for the future. But by a terrible irony Ibsen reveals the incompatibility not merely of these intentions but of the interpretations themselves, so that each reading of the past, except Ella's, and all their purposes with the future become unreal to the measure of their contradiction of each other, while, from this mixture of congruence and con-flict, reality, if we can read it, is evoked.

Rosmersholm is the first play in which supreme achievement in this kind is revealed and the distinctive marks of the late manner are already clear. The plot whose events are the findings brought back from the exploration and revaluation of the past; the profound concern with the inner experience of the mind and with the processes of its self-discovery; the swift, elliptic dialogue at moments of high tension; all these belong to the last phase of Ibsen's writing and are related more or less closely to those parts of the middle plays in which we traced the poetic mode alongside the critical and philosophic. But there are certain advances and variations, here and in the plays that follow, which show that now the poetic mode has prevailed over the philosophic. A long history of mingled outward and inward event, of interacting deeds and decisions, lies behind this play, as behind *Ghosts*. But it is no longer revealed so much by open discussion and analysis as by slight and almost secret impressions. The years before its opening scene might have furnished material for an Elizabethan domestic tragedy. But the substance of this play is the recollection of such a history, its re-assessment in terms of the culminating phase of Rebekka's love, and it is to this exploration that the slight and colourless events of the outward drama prompt her. She works her way backwards under their stimulus, tracing her deeds to their sources, illuminating both deed and motive by her new realization of nobility and love and reinterpreting her present duty by the guidance of this understanding. The character-grouping again, which may seem unchanged, in fact no longer suggests the sculptured image of a theme. It is still a small group of people isolated and closely related, but they are no longer united by their suffering at the hands of a common fate. The close relationship is only accidental; a matter of place and time and physical proximity.

At the centre of the group is the House of Rosmer revealed in John Rosmer, its last descendant, a man of a sensitive and noble imagination, limited in action by his position, but not mentally inactive. The strong but cruder natures of the earlier Rebekka and the Kroll of the time of the play, who destroy between them the peace of his mind but not its lofty self-discipline, reveal by the urgency of their purposes the still and contemplative nature of his. They are in turn illuminated by

Shakespeare and Ibsen as Dramatic Artists

the essentially unimaginative Brendel, in whom rhetoric has dissipated purpose, and by Mortensgaard, in whom the disciplined purpose of expediency has quenched alike passion and vision. None of these could be modified without destroying the effect of the others; the colour of each is intimately dependent upon contrast with and reflection from the colours of all the rest. To all these, the matter-of-fact figure of Mrs Helseth serves as a background, as a reminder of a normal world of unaspiring and unthwarted beings cheerfully untouched by the Rosmer view of life. But these minds are in fact widely separated, half-hostile explorers making partial and momentary contact in the unknown country of the past. The loneliness of self-examination and self-discovery surrounds them, leaving them to guess at each other's positions, hiding them often when they try to approach. And in this lonely exploration we too must discover them by hints as much as by plain revelation, and sometimes by hints that contradict what had seemed to be demonstrable evidence.

In fact, such a subject, with its 'reminiscential evocation', demands a subtle cross-lighting of the characters, so that they may in their turn illuminate each other and the relations between them. For their function is not to demonstrate a theme (though they do in fact discuss many), but to give us a picture of the changing, shifting vicissitudes of the human soul, of its bewildered pilgrimage and, it may be, of its final illumination. To the implications of such plays, whether in terms of character or of event, there is no limit, for their imaginative dimensions reach as far as the thought that they evoke can travel. They have no logic except the logic of poetry, and the mode of poetry has no limitations. We have come a long way from the period of the writing of *Peer Gynt*, but it is clear that, by obscure or it may be devious ways, Ibsen's art has found its way back to and now moves surely in the paths of poetry and power.

One minor but distinctive manifestation of the evocative

mode in Ibsen's drama is to be found in the elliptic dialogue at moments of high tension which, passing over from the great poetic period, becomes more and more frequent in the late plays. This technique in dialogue, so evidently akin to the allusive, evocative revelation of plot and character in these same plays, is to be seen most clearly in the final passages. Here, in *Peer Gynt*, in *Rosmersholm*, in *When We Dead Awaken* and in only less degree in *Brand* and *Little Eyolf*, the resolution of the play is revealed in each case in a passage of dialogue so wholly dependent upon suggestion and the overtones of speech as to be bewildering or almost unintelligible to a reader who has not understood the half-hidden implications in the rest of the play. Of them all, the most noble – and the most obscure to those who have not disposed their imaginations to listen to the evocative overtones – are perhaps the concluding passages of *Peer Gynt* and of *Rosmersholm*. The speeches are simple, brief fragments of utterance, spanning wide gulfs of thought; the two minds in each case seeming to read each other's thought almost without the help of words. The dialogue which reveals this communion of spirit indicates, as it were with touches and hints, the intent and crucial discoveries of two minds swiftly approaching the disclosure of an irradiating truth. No dramatic technique but that of the evocative mode can achieve such revelation as this and no imagination can follow it that has not submitted itself throughout the play to the mode of poetic thought. To describe in 'common words' what flashes from mind to mind between Peer and Solveig or between Rosmer and Rebekka requires several passages of somewhat halting and embarrassed prose. There are passages of dialogue in Shakespeare's plays that have the same quality and make the same demands upon our imaginations; they are to be found here and there too in the other Elizabethan dramatists and in the work of Aeschylus and of Sophocles. Wherever they appear they carry within them the note of high poetry and are the unfailing signs in drama of the evocative and poetic mode.

Shakespeare and Ibsen as Dramatic Artists

To what conclusions have these suggestions been pointing us? To the conclusion that Ibsen, by nature and destiny a poetic dramatist, was born into an age whose preoccupations and mental habits were alien to poetic drama because it had lost the habit of poetic life; that Ibsen's career as an artist reveals a gigantic struggle between his own innate poetic power and a way of life tending more and more to obscure poetic and imaginative reality; that Ibsen alone of all the dramatists of his century had the power to resolve this conflict and that that resolution could only be achieved by accepting the actual and the prosaic and transmuting it into the real and the poetic. The progress of this transmutation may, I think, be traced through his plays from *Peer Gynt* to *Rosmersholm* and its final achievement seen in the last seven plays. In the early stages of this conflict we find the paradoxical figure of the philosopher-dramatist, a major dramatic artist working in non-poetic material and using a partially unpoetic mode. In the final plays the mode is poetic (even if the vehicle is still prose) and the material has been subdued to the purposes of poetry. By a tentative comparison of a few aspects of his technique in two plays with the corresponding technique of Shakespeare we can, I think, perceive where his dramatic art separated from that of his predecessors, Aeschylus, Sophocles, Euripides, and Shakespeare, and how and upon what terms it returned to the way of dramatic poetry.

157

IX

Timon of Athens :
An Unfinished Play [1]

THE PLAY OF *TIMON* has disturbed Shakespeare's critics from an early period and continues to do so. In nearly every respect, from details of style to major characteristics of structure, it is now like, now unlike Shakespeare. Many conjectural explanations of this condition have been offered, but it seems more than usually difficult to reach agreement.[2] Either Shakespeare worked upon an older play of which he retained parts, or he left an unfinished play which was completed by someone else, or the Folio (our only text) is full of cuts and corruptions difficult to explain, or we have merely an unfinished play in which the other 'hand' is negligible or non-existent. These four interpretations are, clearly, not easy to reconcile.

I will not attempt, in these days of restricted space, to recapitulate the excellent work of the bibliographical and textual critics who have discussed the play, for the interpretation to which I incline is not at variance with theirs, and, indeed, rests, as all subsequent criticism must do, upon some

[1] U.E.-F. annotated her copy of this article in preparation for a lecture at Stratford in 1948.

[2] K. Deighton (1905, 1929, *Arden* edition, *Introd.*) sums up the findings of scholars on this and other points to the beginning of this century. E. K. Chambers (*William Shakespeare*, vol. I, pp. 480-4) lists and refers to those that followed until the year 1930. Little has been added since.

of their findings.[1] Nor am I concerned to combat the first three interpretations I mentioned, but, rather, to examine briefly the conclusions to which the fourth may lead us. Sir Edmund Chambers, after mentioning the many theories that have been held, sums up with customary pithiness the position of those who believe in this fourth alternative: 'I do not doubt that it was left unfinished by Shakespeare, and I believe that the real solution of its "problem", indicated long ago by Ulrici and others, is that it is unfinished still.'[2]

It is as an unfinished play, then, that I should like to consider it, a play such as a great artist might leave behind him, roughed out, worked over in part and then abandoned; full of inconsistencies in form and presentation, with fragments (some of them considerable) bearing the unmistakable stamp of his workmanship scattered throughout. Such a text makes it difficult to believe 'another hand' has been at work upon it, for the confusion, whether it affects details of style or the relations of characters and scenes, is precisely what that hand would have been paid to reduce to order.[3] But if we believe that we have here a unique case in the Shakespeare canon, a play

[1] See, again, E. K. Chambers, *William Shakespeare*, vol. I, pp. 480–1. I differ somewhat from Deighton's suggestion (p. xxi) that there was 'some player to whom the editors, failing to find portions known once to have existed, had entrusted the task of putting together the incomplete material', inasmuch as I doubt whether the play had ever reached a state so near completion as this seems to imply. But I would willingly accept the activities of this or some similar functionary in certain of the flat prose scenes which are so undistinguished as to bear the mark of no hand in particular. I differ again from Professor T. M. Parrott's findings in *The Problem of Timon* (1923, *Sh. Ass.*) in that I incline to see more homogeneousness in all but these same scenes and to regard the weaker parts of the play as rough and unfinished drafts by the same hand as the stronger and more nearly finished parts.

[2] *William Shakespeare*, vol. I, p. 482.

[3] It is worth while to remember, in this connection, that there is no evidence that the play was ever produced. Cf. E.K. Chambers, op. cit., 483.

abandoned when only half-worked, and read it through scene by scene in the light of this assumption, we find little which does not seem to be explained thereby.

It is peculiarly fortunate that the first act has in it a large proportion of the play's finished, or relatively finished work. For in this first act the intention of the play, the nature of Shakespeare's mood, something of the dominant theme, are revealed, now clearly now shadowily, but on the whole firmly enough to let us make certain inferences, to use it in some sort as a test of authenticity of style and content in the later parts.

The imagery and the prosody of the opening passages mark them as mature Shakespearean poetry; scenes in which such imagery and such prosody are found must be taken seriously; they will contain, presumably, something that Shakespeare intended to present.[1] The immediate opening up to the entrance of Timon is, it is true, unlike the induction of any other play of his; but we may notice that that is also true of nearly all the plays he wrote after he reached full stature; the theme, in all these, makes its own form. The Jacobean drama offers us a series of notable inductions, and Shakespeare is here, as usual, profoundly original in an age of virtuosos. This passage gives us, moreover, in the poet's allegory, the ironic fore-warning of Timon's fall, a warning which precedes the detailed presentation of his wealth and extravagance that occupies the first two acts, and is picked up at intervals like a melody, sub-ordinate in the early movements of a symphony and becoming dominant at the climax. But it does more than this. It discloses

[1] Here I must differ from T. M. Parrott (op. cit.), who finds the opening weak and unlike Shakespeare's work. Professor Caroline Spurgeon (*Shakespeare's Imagery* (1935), pp. 343-5) finds imagery characteristic of Shakespeare scattered throughout the play, and would, on these grounds, 'assign to Shakespeare (p. 344) a much larger part than has hitherto been attributed to him'. (It is unlike Shakespeare to begin with an allegory. But see Clemen —MS note.)

subtly the deep and penetrating corruption that his wealth has bred. For the poet has a not unworthy idea of the nature and processes of his art (ll. 20–5),[1] and his apostasy is therefore the greater. He is a courtier-poet, one such as other writers as well as Shakespeare had observed, and there are few things that could reveal more swiftly the measure of the world's baseness than this picture of corruption reaching the inner citadel of truth, the integrity of the artist's mind itself. This seems, then, a skilful and significant introduction of the central idea, the hollowness of society and its relations.

This, borne out as it is by the style (the imagery and the blank verse), convinces me that we have here substantially Shakespeare's own introduction, indicating what was his intention. It will be wise, therefore, to accept as also part of Shakespeare's intention whatever in the rest of the play is clearly related to this, in mood, in action or in style.

The latter part of this scene (from the entrance of Apemantus) offers some difficulties, but they are not insuperable. It is certainly a thin patch of writing. There are very few touches of live imagery or music, and these (257–61, 289–92) occur in the later part. Even Apemantus, afterwards an integral part of the play's content and structure affecting both the outer and the inner action, lacks sinew here and is no more than a kind of conventional Diogenes crossed with a little diluted Thersites. I can see no artistic reason for this flatness, but we must admit that there is some, though not so much, of the same kind in other plays that are psychologically related to *Timon* – in *All's Well*, in *Measure for Measure*, and even in

[1] Line references are to the Oxford edition of Shakespeare's works, ed. W. J. Craig (1913). With the poet's demeanour here should, of course, be compared that of v. 1, particularly ll. 51, et seq.; with his theory of art we may compare Theseus's (*M.S.N.D.*, v. i, 7–17) and perhaps Tamburlaine's (II *Tamb.*, v. ii, 114–20), though this last is a little complicated by a hopelessly corrupt text. But Shakespeare's most significant comment on poetic character is to be found in Sonnet CX.

M

Troilus and Cressida.[1] One might venture the suggestion that
this part was roughed out and not finished: it compares badly
with the first half of the scene, which was either worked over
after roughing out or written more eagerly in the first instance.
For one reason or for the other, the earlier seems more fully
imagined and so more finished.

There is nothing in the second scene to make us withdraw.
In fact, the design of the outward action seems sound and
broadly based up to the end of the act. As a first act, that is,
this one does its work. If the next four had been lost we
should have no reason to suspect artistic confusion or collapse
in what was to follow. We are clearly promised shock and
catastrophe. So close at hand do we feel them that we might
guess the main theme of the play, the inner action which the
outer events would reveal, to be the effect of that shock on the
mind and philosophy of the man who was to suffer it. Looking
forward at this point without knowing the rest of the play,
we might anticipate some kinship with *Troilus and Cressida*
and more with *Lear*; the experience of the central figure will
be such, perhaps, as to image some universal law whose
operation he discovers and interprets, as does Lear. Even a few
of the details of Timon's conduct suggest a likeness between his
character and Lear's at a similar stage of their fortunes; auto-
cracy and imperiousness tinge his generosity with insolence.[2]
Some resemblance between their experiences may therefore be
intended; a headlong career, to be brought up suddenly by a

[1] Cf. E. K. Chambers, op. cit., pp. 451-2 and 455-6. *Troilus and Cressida* is
not strictly analogous to *Timon* in this respect, for the use of prose there is
usually functional, having a clearly discernible artistic intention; it may
serve, therefore, to indicate rather a resemblance in underlying purpose,
clearly expressed in the earlier play and confusedly in the later.

[2] We may notice especially, I. ii. 13-14 and 165-239, passim. There are,
besides this, unexplained touches of cynicism in the earlier scene (157-61,
172-4) which are perhaps best understood as hints of psychic unbalance in
Timon which we would do well to keep in mind from the beginning.

Timon of Athens

change of fortune; the reason unseated; the character, ill-balanced already, being totally unfitted to survive the shock.

Moreover, two of the chief characters that appear here are built strongly into the play and do, in fact, maintain their shape and position later when much else goes to wreck. Apemantus's mood seems at first to run counter to that of the play, in churlish opposition. But when the crisis has turned the tide, it is found to be the dominant stream that carries all with it; as the play goes on, there is a slowly deepening power and increasing relevance in his speech which indicates design. Flavius, again, is planted firmly in the action both of events and of ideas. He has, moreover, the special function of uttering in more precise definition the vague warnings and threats of the poet's allegory at the beginning. This theme, which we are never allowed to escape for long, has clearly been foreseen from the beginning.

But beside these indications of deliberate planning of the functional relations of the characters to the main theme, we notice signs of unfinished work in the details of this act. The broken and irregular lines, the patchwork effect of many even of the finest speeches, have long troubled Shakespeare's critics here. They are indeed extremely difficult to explain in terms of any kind of corruption known to bibliographical critics; with the best will in the world, I cannot see how playhouse additions or excisions or the most illegible palimpsest that was ever handed to a compositor in the form of a prompt-copy could have produced just this condition.[1] But I can see without any difficulty at all how a man who was roughing out a scene might leave a speech in this form: it is to my mind as strong evidence as we can find that whoever wrote these passages did

[1] But see T. M. Parrott, *The Problem of Timon* (*Sh. Ass.* 1923), for a very different interpretation of this evidence, with which, in all respect, I find myself unable to agree. Yet another interpretation, with which also I cannot bring myself into agreement, is that of Dixon Wecter (*Shakespeare's Purpose in Timon, P.M.L.A.*, xliii, 1928).

not finish them. And the presence of many such in the play, and in speeches of undeniable majesty and power, is likewise the best evidence I could ask that Shakespeare wrote the rest of the play also, and, similarly, left it unfinished. At the risk of being over-explicit, I will cite a passage (actually from a later scene) which embodies the characteristics of these broken speeches wherever they occur.

ALCIBIADES

My lord,—

FIRST SENATOR

You cannot make gross sins look clear;	1
To revenge is no valour, but to bear.	2

ALCIBIADES

My lords, then, under favour, pardon me,	3
If I speak like a captain.	4
Why do fond men expose themselves to battle,	5
And not endure all threats? sleep upon't,	6
And let the foes quietly cut their throats	7
Without repugnancy? If there be	8
Such valour in the bearing, what make we	9
Abroad? [why] then, women are more valiant	10
That stay at home, if bearing carry it,	11
And the ass more captain than the lion, the felon	12
Loaded with irons wiser than the judge,	13
If wisdom be in suffering. O my lords!	14
As you are great, be pitifully good:	15
Who cannot condemn rashness in cold blood?	16
To kill, I grant, is sin's extremest gust;	17
But, in defence, by mercy, 'tis most just	18
To be in anger is impiety;	19
But who [is] that man that is not angry?	20
Weigh but the crime with this.[1]	21

[1] *Timon*, III. v. 37–59.

Timon of Athens

The power both of the language and of the music of individual lines or groups of lines is unmistakable. The speech is a succession of units, sometimes a line and a half, sometimes two, sometimes as many as seven.[1] Very often these units are made up of a half line followed by one or more complete lines and concluded by another half line, sometimes the bracketing of an interjection would restore the flow of a line.[2] These passages, in other words, are jottings, thoughts that form in the writer's mind as prosodic units, but are not yet related prosodically so as to form a verse paragraph or even a continuous succession of blank verse lines. The breaks that occur at the ends of lines 4 and 20, or in the middle of certain lines (6, 8, 10, 12)[3] where the foot and a half or two feet after the pause clearly belong to the thought and movement of the next unit, bear, to my mind, less suggestion of corruption after writing than of writing which has not been re-digested and rendered harmonious. A characteristic of these passages wherever they occur is that prosodic units are, as here, simultaneously units of thought or imagery, complete in themselves even when imperfectly related to their neighbours and to the whole speech.[4] Who, that has ever written blank verse in any condition below that of complete collection and concentration, has not experienced this preliminary rush of isolated fragments of music and thought? We may agree that Shakespeare's artistic experience cannot without irreverence be interpreted in terms of any but a very few of those upon record. Nevertheless, some likeness of process may perhaps be presumed.

Taking together, then, these various indications from the first act of *Timon*, I incline to think that what we have here is Shakespeare's work in varying degrees of completion and at varying levels of imaginative intensity but still substantially

[1] As in ll. 3-4, 1-2, 13-19.   [2] As in 6-8, 10, and 20.

[3] My numbering is, of course, purely for convenience in reference and has no relation to the text.

[4] Contrast *T.N.K.* – MS note.

the first act that he planned, with some of the later action and the main theme already in his mind, and that parts of the design here conceived were strongly enough formed to emerge firm and powerful throughout the play. I think also that he was experimenting with structure; again, as in *Troilus and Cressida*, attempting a theme so original that the form it dictated must inevitably be revolutionary.[1] What was the experiment in this case and what the consequent form it may be hard to discover.[2] It was certainly not a repetition of that of *Troilus and Cressida*, though it may well have been an advance from that position. And, where that of *Troilus and Cressida* was just within his power to compass and ours to follow, it may be that this of *Timon* was just beyond both.

The second act, however, shows as yet no signs of weakness. Where the first act had been extended and in parts almost leisurely, as fits the induction to an inner action of vast scope, this second act is correspondingly rapid; the audience may be presumed to have grasped what is involved and the action can go forward. Its relation to the preceding act seems sound enough, too, in actual plotting; the change in the direction of Timon's fortunes, for which we have been consciously or unconsciously prepared, is now presented. There are flat passages again, it is true, but the mixture of tediousness with vigorous commentary in II. ii. 73–129, has the same function as similar passages in *Measure for Measure*, it reveals a background that we must take into account if we are to perceive justly the relations of values in the play. And the later part of the second scene (133–242) we can by no means dismiss, for some of the verbal music and its imagery is as powerful as in any play

[1] The theme in *Troilus and Cressida* is, I believe, that of disintegration and disjunction itself, one which in its very nature passes almost beyond the scope of drama. (Cf. the essay in *The Frontiers of Drama* – K.M.)

[2] Nor is it the purpose of this article to discuss either. One of the more interesting modern interpretations is that of Professor Wilson Knight in *The Wheel of Fire* (1930).

of this period; here at least we have finished or relatively
finished work.

But one thing disturbs us in this act, our first meeting with
a conspicuous and inexplicable loose end in the character of the
Fool. Although the passage in which he appears is well enough
written, he is not built into the play. We do not know who
he is or where he comes from. We hardly know to whom he
belongs. And he disappears never to appear again. We are
forced to one of two assumptions: either that he ceased to be
part of Shakespeare's design by a change of intention after
this scene, or that the scenes or passages in which his function
and relation to the play would have appeared were never
written or were lost. He is the first, but not the last disturbing
element of this kind that we shall find in the play.

The third act gives us, on the whole, an impression of
planning, but after the first three scenes we come upon more
uneven work than before and upon downright inconsistency.
The first three scenes, however, stand well together as a group.
I think we can feel in them Shakespeare's design even if they
are sometimes unfinished in detail. The masterly skill of long
experience lies behind the treatment of the parallel episodes of
Lucullus, Lucius, Sempronius, and Ventidius, so handled, in
different ways, as to avoid repetition while building up the
impression of accumulation, to reveal at once the individuality
of the characters and the monotony of their behaviour. No
dramatic novice wrote this scene. There are several long prose
passages in the first two scenes, but they all seem to some
extent functional; the prose, that is to say, conveys an effect
that verse would not so well achieve and moves naturally into
verse in Shakespeare's accustomed manner. The broken verse
'jottings' that we have already noticed appear again, sometimes (i. 55–67, ii. 72–95) in a chain of fine images and prosodic
units that are as they stand skeletons of verse paragraphs. One
detail that first becomes noticeable here is perhaps worth
bearing in mind, the brief references to 'the gods', that might

be passed over as mere mechanical phrases, were it not that they recur as does an iterative image and culminate in a passage of inescapable significance in a later act.[1] The very presence of such a recurrent minor theme, the more indicative in that it is unobtrusive, suggests the continuing presence also of a presiding idea of which it is the momentary revelation.

The act as a whole gives, as I suggested, an impression of being planned; but there is no consistent carrying through of the plan as in the first and to some degree in the second. Apart from the fact that the first three scenes are much more closely grouped than those that follow and that the climax in the sixth scene seems only a sketch, falling far short of the expectation that has been raised in us, there is the strange and startling incursion made by the fifth scene. This scene has given the commentators more trouble than any other in the play. Professor Boas[2] long ago declared strongly in favour of Shakespeare's authorship of this scene and there does not seem any reason, in the light of what has been said since, to reject it. It is a fine Shakespearean scene: the difficulty lies not in its quality but in its function.[3] Apart from 'jottings' (of the kind we have already noticed twice) interwoven with the otherwise highly wrought verse, its condition could be called 'finished'. But to what purpose was it finished? Questions beset us as we read. What is this trial that is in progress?

[1] See III. iii. 37; iv. 26, 78; v. 119; vi. 78, 85, 90, 92. Also IV. i. 37; ii. 4, 41; iii. 26, 30, 71, 72, 104, 139, 389, 467, 488, 504–6, culminating in this last passage in *Timon's* speech to Flavius:

> Forgive my general and exceptless rashness
> Ye perpetual-sober gods.

[2] *Shakespeare and his Predecessors* (1896), pp. 502, 503.

[3] Commentators are not entirely agreed upon the quality of the scene and the proportion which they are willing to attribute to Shakespeare. T. M. Parrott (op. cit.), sees stronger evidence here of Chapman's hand than of Shakespeare's. But I think the majority of critics at the present day would give it to Shakespeare.

For whom is Alcibiades pleading? What has happened? And when? What has it to do with what goes before? Or, as we are presently in a position to ask, with what follows? It tumbles suddenly into the action with the bewildering inconsequence of an episode in a dream and its power and its vividness only strengthen this impression. Worse still, perhaps, they convince us that Shakespeare wrote this scene with considerable enthusiasm; he either cared enough about it to work over it until it was coherent and vigorous, or he came to it with a measure of artistic delight great enough to carry it through, clear and shapely, at the first writing.

Can we make any conjecture about this scene which will throw light not only on what is to follow, but upon the state of the whole play? Of many that have been made, one, I think, comes near to solving this dilemma of a scene characteristically Shakespearean in style which has hardly any relation to the main action of the play in which it appears.

Either, it is clear, the scene belongs to some alternative action or sub-plot which was finally discarded, in which case it has presumably strayed into the text as did, according to one theory, the re-written passages of *Love's Labour's Lost*, or it is an essential part of the action of the play as it was planned and its supporting scenes are lost or were never written. It may be noticed that, though it has as it stands no connection with the preceding action of the play, it has some kinship with the theme, for the changes are rung here, as all through the play, on the contrast between generous friendship and ingratitude. If it was a part of Shakespeare's design, nothing remains to confirm this or to show how it was to be related to the foregoing scenes except one or two hints in Alcibiades' speech (IV. iii. 94–5) and in the senators' embassy to Timon (V. i, especially 152–69), which suggest that it was Timon himself who had committed the murder and was the subject of the trial. This of course presupposes that a supporting scene or passage earlier in the act has been lost (or never written) as well as the necessary references that must have followed. But it does at least, if we can agree to it, clear away several difficulties. This scene, characteristically Shakespearean as it is in style, might, in that case, have been functional, taking up its place in the action of the play; the relationship of Alcibiades to the rest of the play could thereupon become firm and coherent instead of disturbing us as it does by its inconclusiveness; the action of the final scenes of the play would take on a substance and a coherence that it badly lacks, and, in fact, the whole of Act V could be related to the main action. It becomes increasingly difficult to resist the idea that a series of passages is missing, containing such essential parts of the story as would have made the structure of the last three acts solid by relating Timon clearly to Alcibiades and both to Athenian politics. Such an interpretation even offers us the possibility of a climax related to that of *Coriolanus* (a cognate play) reversing the choice and the direction taken by the action there.

The fourth act presents no such interruptions to the scheme of the play. There are several parts that we accept at sight, not only because their style bears the authentic marks of Shakespeare's workmanship, but also because they are related to the supposed plan of the whole (whose working-out is now, admittedly, becoming a little erratic). Timon's soliloquy in the first scene is one of these; it is, in addition, closely related to *Troilus and Cressida* (another cognate play) in thought and even in many details of its imagery. The second scene is less strongly characterized, but there is nothing in it actually suspicious; the broken verse is of the kind that is now familiar and the imagery is sometimes powerful. The allusions to 'the gods' that run like a thread through the later acts appear again and link it both with the third act and with the following scene. The last scene of this act is the most important in the play, as it stands, and there is no reason to suppose that it was not the climax in the design. The full working-out of the thought, fuller than in any other part, and the potency of the imagery, which is not only cogent and impressive, but significant of the main lines of thought throughout, convince me that here again we have something which is substantially Shakespeare's intention. It relates itself closely to *Troilus and Cressida* on the one hand and to *Lear* on the other, the two plays which seem to stand nearest to *Timon* in their mood and interpretation.

The fifth act is again uneven. So erratic is the relating of its parts that we sometimes feel as if we are reading a mixture of two different plays. Yet all through it[1] are the signs of mature writing which make us hesitate to say that it has not been touched by Shakespeare.[2] Timon's speeches arise naturally out of what has gone before, but the sudden incursion of the senators[3] and their control of the final scenes is hardly related at all to the original design, and the matter here is not solid or potent enough to be the culmination of what has been so powerfully planned. Again, we are strongly tempted to assume some missing scenes grouped round and relating to III. v which might have connected that scene with these, and these, thereby, to the whole plan. We cannot help, that is, the suspicion that the condition of the play is more than a matter of scenes that have not been worked over and a minor character, like the fool, who has not been clearly related. For from the middle of the third act there are major inconsistencies, most noticeable in the unexplained appearance of III. v, always involving Alcibiades and the Athenians and ending in the structural disjunction of the fifth act. As we have reason to believe that the plot was firmly designed, we can only assume that the design is not fairly represented by what remains.

If this were the end of the problem it would be a relatively

---

[1] With the exception of the scene (iii) of ten lines which achieves a degree of irrelevance unsurpassed even in this play, being incongruous in style and thought, superfluous in the plot, and contradictory in the one matter (l. 3) which appears to offer some relationship with iv. 65–73. I make no claims upon this scene.

[2] Especially, perhaps, i. 144–233; ii and iv.   [3] i. 121–233.

simple one and there would, perhaps, be no need to re-state it. But we have avoided mention so far of the greatest weakness in the play, that which gives us more ground for uneasiness than all of these – the character of Timon.[1] This goes deep into the fabric of the play and we cannot explain it away by saying that something has been lost or not written or not worked-over. This is a matter of conception, not of working-out. For our complaint concerning Timon is not that we do not see enough of him, but that, in spite of the length of time during which he occupies the stage, he fails to leave a deep, coherent impression of his personality. And this is at its worst in the first two acts which we found no reason for supposing unfinished or unrepresentative of Shakespeare's intention regarding the central theme. Timon here is negative. There *is* no individuality.[2] There is, it is true, a picture of great wealth and extravagant squandering, but this is not fit to support either so mighty a theme as is foreshadowed at the beginning, or a conversion such as the mood of the fourth and fifth acts presuppose. We may say perhaps that we have there, after all, only one aspect of Timon. To which we may well be tempted to reply, Where, then, are the others? Extravagance was, it is true, a single aspect of certain magnificent figures dear to Elizabethan and Jacobean writers, the great Italian nobles of the Renascence and their English equivalents, Wolsey, Raleigh, Essex. But Timon is not magnificent; magnificence presupposes other qualities also; power, purpose, the capacity for lofty if contaminated design, a wide variety of enthusiasms and richness of personality.[3] Put Timon beside Alexander VI,

[1] I am aware that in what follows I join issue with Professor Wilson Knight (*The Wheel of Fire*), who, in his highly suggestive and subtle study of Timon, interprets him as a product of humanism and the 'flower of human aspiration'. I readily agree that this is what he well might have been, but I fail to detect the actual evidence in the play.

[2] See Pettet for different interpretation – MS note.

[3] Further significance seen by Pettet – MS note.

Timon of Athens

Lorenzo di Medici, Henry VIII, or Raleigh, and what loftiness of purpose, imagination, or liberality is there in him? Put him beside Antony or Lear and where is the splendour with which Shakespeare could, when he wished, invest a figure? The Timon of the first acts has little but extravagance and a kind of isolated self-assurance.

And this impression of negation and isolation is deepened, not dissipated, as we look closer. We do not know him and we do not know about him. Indeed, we begin to wonder whether he is not, himself, the greatest of the unrelated elements in the play. For he is only real by reason of his continual presence. Apart from that, he is hardly better built into his society on the grand scale than the fool is on a small scale. What, after all, do we know of his circumstances and relations, past and present, compared with all that we know or can divine of Hamlet, Lear, or Coriolanus? If we begin to ask ourselves some of the questions to which Shakespeare generally provides unobtrusive answers, how many of them can we in fact answer? What is the source of his wealth; is it inherited or acquired? If inherited, how long has he had complete control of it? If acquired, by what means did he acquire it? Who were his parents and when did they die – if indeed they are dead? How long has he been an orphan – if indeed he is? Has he no blood relations? How and where was he brought up? If he was out of touch with courts, why are we not told so? If in the court, why is he so little aware of its pitfalls? How old is he? If he is very young, why has he not some of the characteristics of youth? Why, above all, is he not in love? If he is of mature age, why is he such a fool? And why again, in that case, does he bear no signs of the experience he must have met, above all, the acute knowledge of man that palace intrigue would have given to a strong intelligence? Shakespeare, who could reveal with such delicate discrimination the precise effect that the court of Cymbeline has had on each personality that has come within its influence, did not lack the skill to do this for

Timon, upon whose fortunes court-life is the determining influence.

Why, then, did Shakespeare, who elsewhere allows us to discover details of this kind, who builds a character into its society and uses those ties to reveal its operations, not do so here? Why did the poet who surrounded Hamlet in a web of circumstance give us this man who not only has no past but has no close connections in his present world, no parents, brothers, sisters, wife, mistress, or friend? How can we imagine in Timon a man of strong and mature personality when he has no strong relationships in the present and shows no signs of their having moulded him in the past? And such a theme as this play seemed to design can only, we need hardly say, be imaged in a personality of the greatest power, the widest scope and the highest spirit and intelligence: his kinsmen, in the plays that lie nearest in mood, are, after all, Hamlet, Ulysses, Troilus, Lear.

Shakespeare may, it is true, have intended to throw the character into isolation, but it is hard to believe that, if he had, he would not have indicated this with a fulness and clarity that left no room for mistake in those two relatively finished early acts. Hamlet is isolated; it is a part of the play's design that he should be. But we know it beyond mistake and we know how it has come about. Moreover the people who contribute to it are themselves so deeply imagined and so clearly revealed that we see precisely what was the limitation in Gertrude, in Ophelia, in Horatio, in Laertes, in Rosencrantz, in Guildenstern, that frustrated communication. Regan, Goneril, Cornwall, again, have clear individuality to give weight and precision to their functions in the play. But unlike *Hamlet*, unlike *Lear*, the play of *Timon* does not endow its minor characters with the function of focusing, by their nature and actions, our thought and attention on the central figure.

Shakespeare's intention may not have been very near any of those that I have somewhat boldly indicated here. But to admit that is not to explain away the two great weaknesses in the structure that we have here suggested: that the character of Timon is inadequate to the theme and that the action does not knit together his fate and that of the other people in the play. We have no impression of greatness in Timon commensurate with the tragic experience of which he is apparently the responsible exponent, and we miss the familiar Shakespearean relating of character to society and circumstance which itself, in the Shakespearean system, gives rise to action. Yet, since all these weaknesses are to be found in scenes which in other ways seem part of an ordered design, we must suppose that we have here a character which has not been deeply imagined. Shakespeare, who could reveal with penetrating rapidity the individuality of Albany or even of the murderers in *Macbeth*, has here put before us at great length a character which, but for a few violent passions and harshly outlined traits, is colourless and neutral.

Timon is an unfinished play in a far deeper sense than that which is implied by saying Shakespeare left off writing before he had set down all that was in his mind. It *is* unfinished in this way also, it is true. But, what matters more, it is unfinished in conception. We can explain the broken verse and the loose ends easily; we can explain nearly as easily the imperfections of the plot; we can even isolate the main theme and show how unworthy of it is the working-out in the later acts. What we cannot explain is our impression that this play is indeed 'Hamlet without the Prince of Denmark', the character of Timon being often a blank. Here is that rarest of all weaknesses in Shakespeare's work, an element which is not wholly functional; a character which does not convince us, upon inspection, that, given its nature and these events, the resultant action presented to us is inevitable. Dare we suggest that, for some reason at which we can only dimly guess, Shakespeare chose the wrong character to support his theme, and, consequently, the wrong outer action as the image of the inner

Shakespeare the Dramatist

action? This obviously leaves us as far as ever from real knowledge of the cause of the play's collapse, but it may suggest one reason why it came to a standstill, was 'unfinished' in the more limited and technical sense also. How Shakespeare, with his unsurpassed artistic and psychological sureness, came to make so colossal a blunder is a matter on which we dare not conjecture. Were there other plays which also miscarried, which have not survived? Did this survive against his intention? All that we can say with any certainty is that here is a design not wholly comprehended and subdued by the shaping spirit of imagination.[1]

[1] At the end of the article is a note for guidance in converting the 1942 article into a lecture: 'Apologise for still holding the same opinion. Recapitulate position. Take account of fresh material since my 1942. (A) Collins 1946. Discuss. (B) Pettet 1947. Accept. . . . Modification of my position of '42, admitting relevance of Pettet's material at certain points.' The articles referred to are: A. S. Collins, *R.E.S.* (1946), pp. 96–108; E. C. Pettet, *R.E.S.* (1947), pp. 321–36.

X

The Two Noble Kinsmen

I PROPOSE TO DISCUSS IN this note only those parts of *Two Noble Kinsmen* to which mystery attaches: the parts, that is, which are not universally accepted as Fletcher's. And in computing these I shall take a relatively conservative position, such as that originally suggested by Littledale, and include I. i (41 to the end); parts of I. ii, iii, iv; II; III. i, ii; most of IV. iii; V. i (20 to the end); V. iii, iv (except 99 to 113).

It would be interesting to know how many readers of this play have gone through the same series of reactions as Spalding, Fleay, and Furnivall; convinced on a first reading that the group of scenes sometimes known as 'A' *must* be Shakespeare's work, doubtful on a second reading some years later and finally convinced, after another interval of time, that it could not be. When I went over the play again recently I found myself for a brief period holding four mutually incompatible convictions: First that the play could not possibly be Shakespeare's, second that it was too much like his work to be anyone else's, third that it was the product of an unholy alliance between Chapman and Beaumont, both temporarily intoxicated by Shakespeare's later tragic style, and fourth that it was the only surviving play of an unknown genius who had read nothing for some six weeks but Shakespeare's mature tragedies. Setting aside the more frivolous of these suggestions, I find myself back at the first position, that it cannot possibly be Shakespeare's work; in agreement, that is, with Tucker Brooke's admirable brief study of 1908 and in disagreement with E. K. Chambers's verdict of 1930, which is but a suspension of disbelief.

But conviction is no argument and something nearer a

Shakespeare the Dramatist

reasonable statement must be made. The Stationers' Register entry and the title-page ascription of 1634 are, as is generally admitted, of too late date to convince us of Shakespeare's authorship in the absence of evidence from the play itself, and still less able in the presence of contrary evidence from within. The time is ripe for a fresh consideration of all the arguments that have been advanced in the last twenty years of the nineteenth century and the first thirty-five of this – from those of Littledale, that is, through Tucker Brooke's, Dugdale Sykes', W. J. Lawrence's, and E. K. Chambers's to Alfred Hart's. There has been pretty common agreement that the play is not homogeneous, that certain scenes (including as a rule those I have just mentioned) are of a kind to raise suspicions of Shakespeare's authorship, while the remainder are not. At this point agreement ceases and various techniques have been used, various tests applied, to determine the authorship, for the most part of A (the possibly Shakespearean parts), but sometimes of B (the rest).

I propose, with your permission, to speak, for these few minutes, of one kind of evidence only, the evidence for or against Shakespeare's authorship which can be drawn from the quality and characteristics of the play *as a play*; that is, the aesthetic evidence. I think that one of the tasks that remains for contemporary scholarship in this field is a thorough and systematic investigation of the aesthetic evidence, which will, I submit, be found overwhelmingly convincing when so examined. The undertaking is formidable. But with your permission, I propose to indicate to-day the lines along which such an investigation might properly be made, in respect of style, treatment of character, the foundations of action, the relation of character and action, and the emergent thought. I think such an investigation would have to watch closely not only Shakespeare's demeanour in these matters in some two or three authentic plays which should serve as controls – *Cymbeline*, *Winter's Tale*, perhaps *Henry VIII*, but also the somewhat intricate relations with *Pericles* and *Timon*. The condition of

178

each of these seems at some point curiously like that of *Two Noble Kinsmen*, but that likeness resolves itself in each case, on nearer inspection, into a mirage. In this, as in much else, this brilliant and baffling play of *Two Noble Kinsmen* shows itself a masterpiece of theatrical virtuosity precisely in that power of creating an illusion of reality where no reality is.

I have suggested that there should be a close comparative analysis of the characteristics of this play in respect of style, treatment of character, conduct of plot and relating of characters and plot and of subject and theme. I suggest these only because they are the rough categories which every scholar of dramatic aesthetics uses in some form or other in order to define and separate various aspects of technique. No mere analysis, of course, that is not followed by synthesis constitutes a full critical survey. The emergent work of art (or the emergent something which fails to be a work of art) is in the last resort the criterion of authorship. But the analytic method serves us particularly well in studying a play such as this, in which the skill of the author seems to be deployed mainly in order to dazzle and bemuse us.

Much has been written about the style of *Two Noble Kinsmen*, and rightly, since it is the vocabulary, the syntax, the imagery, and the verbal music that are chiefly responsible for what has been called the 'undeniably Shakespearean tone' which might be the mask of Shakespeare's own hand, but is more probably a 'strong Shakespearean reminiscence'. Each of these aspects of the stylistic technique must, I submit, be examined closely in four ways. In the first place the most notable words (especially those of a striking and individual kind, of which there are several), notable turns of sentence structure, the separate images, and the most arresting cadences and prosodic units must be considered in themselves against the background of recognized processes as we find them in the authentic plays. Then their relation to each other, the collaborations, as it were, between these different aspects of stylistic

Shakespeare the Dramatist

technique must be examined. If no collaboration, or insufficient relation, be found, that in itself will be a fact of some significance. Then each of these cases and the groups they form must be examined afresh in relation to the purpose of the play; their function in the work of art, or the failure of function, must be diagnosed. Finally all these groups and the conclusions arrived at in the first three examinations must be reviewed in the special relation they bear to the relevant parts of *Pericles*, *Timon*, and *Henry VIII*. Moreover, in the third of these groups (the images), the methods devised by Caroline Spurgeon for the use of imagery as a test of authorship should be borne in mind; iterative imagery or image clusters (both striking features of Shakespeare's work) may or may not be present here. Each of these investigations is a considerable task and must be the work of a specialist in its own field. But if the work required is, as I have suggested, formidable, the findings would, I am convinced, be definite.

The same method, or something like it, is called for in investigating the treatment of character in the play. Here the evidence may sometimes be confused, if only because the passages under question cannot be isolated so completely from the parts of the play which are generally agreed to be Fletcher's. But we find on looking closer that this only affects one half of the evidence. Choice and grouping of characters, that important side of the treatment of character which has been called the spatial aspect of the play, must indeed be affected by collaboration, since there must presumably be substantial agreement between the two writers as to which characters to introduce and of what kind and where. But on the other side of this part of a dramatist's technique – that of the penetration into the nature of a given character and revelation of its responses, motives, experience, and, it may be, development – one partner in a loose collaboration may well have freedom enough to reveal his own accustomed technique in a single scene. Many of us are assured that Shakespeare does find this necessary elbow

180

room in the relevant parts of *Pericles*. Admitting, then, that we cannot well look for signs of Shakespeare's hand in the grouping of characters, we may yet do so in the treatment of individual figures, and here again we shall consider these characters, first, one at a time, against the background of evidence afforded by the plays as a whole, and then in relation to each other and to the purposes of the play. We shall apply to them also, that is to say, the crucial test of function. In the same way we shall investigate first the conduct of the action, the plot as a plot – at which point, if there is collaboration, we shall certainly be hampered by its effects – and then the all important relation of character and action, the repercussion of event and character upon each other, which is one of the final tests of structural validity in a work of dramatic art.

Now it is clearly not within my province here to consider all these four aspects of dramatic technique in the three or four relations possible to each, nor is it my intention even to begin to inflict such an analysis upon my audience. All that I consider it possible to do to-day is to give an illustration of the kind of evidence that I find in each case and then jump straight to the conclusion that I have drawn.

Of the four or five aspects of the style which may be considered, vocabulary is perhaps the least likely to give us conclusive evidence of Shakespeare's authorship. There are a rather surprising number of words here that seem unusual even to the general reader – they do not, that is to say, occur in the works of the other dramatists or in Shakespeare's other plays. This was sometimes taken to be strong evidence against Shakespeare's authorship (though admittedly it argued also against Fletcher's share in A). But in 1934 Alfred Hart, with a pretty and neat organization of his statistics, showed that 'a high proportion of words found in one play only' is in fact characteristic of Shakespeare's vocabulary, and deftly turned to cogent evidence in favour of his authorship what had seemed one of the strongest points against it. Nevertheless, I cannot

Shakespeare the Dramatist

believe with Hart that Shakespeare's authorship is established by this demonstration; those of us who see in this play a dazzling imitation of Shakespeare's hand rather than Shakespeare's hand itself have always been prepared to admit that it is 'imitation' in the Aristotelian sense. In an argument such as Hart's it is natural to emphasize the seemingly Shakespearean usage of these unique words rather than those which seem equally un-Shakespearean.

Syntax, cadence, and imagery go deeper into the fabric of a man's thought, and it is here that the imitator achieves his most surprising – and, be it admitted, imaginative – feats of reproduction: sentence-structure and balance of clauses that are like those of *Pericles, Cymbeline, Winter's Tale, Tempest, Henry VIII* at first glance, and quite unlike when they are dissected; cadences that deceive us by their harmony with the verbal music of one or other of these five plays until we notice that they are in unison with several of Fletcher's and Ford's; imagery that surprises by a fine excess, but turns out to have more brilliance than potency, to dazzle, rather than to illuminate. There is, moreover, a relation between these three; and we must define the extent to which syntactical peculiarities or eccentricities modulate the music of a passage or appear to modulate it, or an unusual expansion and contraction of rhythm, a spondaic feminine ending (like Webster's) in a run-on passage works seeming havoc with the lucidity of what turns out upon analysis to be a normal piece of syntax or a plain and superficial image. This trick of playing off syntax against cadence and imagery against both is much in Chapman's manner and perhaps helps to explain the vigour with which his claims have sometimes been put forward. But I ask you to bear in mind such passages as Act I, scene ii, ll. 18–46 or 104–21 or Act I, scene iv, ll. 32–50, and consider again, in respect of the three aspects of style that I have briefly indicated, what results, first from the analysis of each and then from synthesis and re-examination of their interplay and mutual relation, and

182

say whether either the detail or the resultant can be strictly related to Shakespeare's work.

The claims of the pseudo-Shakespearean style must be combated on their own grounds, and without references to other aspects of the play's content and form. But the persistent shallowness of characterization in Emilia, the superficial novelty in Hippolyta, which never fulfils its promise, the false motivation, the evoking of emotion by undramatic methods – all these cut deeper into the art of the play and reveal habits of thought and technique so unlike Shakespeare's that they have shaken the confidence of many critics who had been convinced or half-convinced by the style. In the same way, the conduct of the plot is unlike that of an artist whose known processes have the economy of great architecture: the first, flamboyant scene bears, as Tucker Brooke points out, no strict relation to the sequent plot. From such observations we should not hope to find an organic relation of plot and character or of plot and motive. Tragic inevitability will not emerge from this hodge-podge of event and situation and we too often surprise our author in the act of faking it to believe that Shakespeare could have had control of the main lines of this play. At the end of Act V, scene iii, the faking takes the form of a dialogue full of pathetic affirmations of the pitiable fatality of the situation, which serve only to reveal the insecurity of the stresses in its structure; there is no more genuine necessity in the main action than in that spectacular opening scene. When all is said, the burying of bones, a sacred and compelling necessity to Antigone, cannot be made to release the same force of passion and action for the seventeenth century, and, from beginning to end, that scene is a brilliant piece of virtuosity labouring unsuccessfully to conceal this hard fact.

Such thought as the play has, which is far less than it appears to have, lacks altogether that depth, that simultaneous hold upon intellect and imagination, which we recognize in any work of Shakespeare's designing. There is at once more explicit statement

183

Shakespeare the Dramatist

alike of sentiment and of reflection and less implication of coherent reading of life than we find in the total impression of
Pericles or even *Timon*. Fake values at work in the underlying
thought emerge in the characters as false motivation, to reinforce the theatrical tone of the situations and the episodic nature
of the structure. And all these weaknesses are screened by a
bewildering brilliance of style and a facile and dexterous release
of the shallower emotions. It is hardly worth while to search
behind this screen for a theme, and still less for a valid relation between theme and subject – that ultimate test of dramatic virility.

But all the categories that I have so hastily indicated (short
of this one) should, I consider, be examined in some detail if the
claims of the doubtful scenes to be regarded as Shakespeare's
workmanship are to be refuted. If we now reverse the order in
which we have examined these, we reach, I suggest, the
following conclusion.

The planning of the play is unlike Shakespeare's known
designs, first in the underlying thought from which springs its
reading of life, second in the absence of that interlocking of
motive and event, character and plot, which is one of the basic
criteria of great dramatic art, third in the nature of its style,
the brilliance of which is startling, not illuminating; explosive,
not imaginative or evocative. It is upon the style that those
claims have in general been most firmly based and indeed our
author's knowledge of Shakespeare is superb, going far deeper
than mere reminiscence – though there is reminiscence in
abundance – to simulate the habit of his sentence structure, of
his verbal music, of his imagery and of his vocabulary. But that
it should be the work of Shakespeare is to me incredible.
Apart from the theatrical over-heightening at all levels of the
technique that I have already named, and the specific unlikeness
that is revealed as each is examined in turn, there is the inherent difficulty of explaining precisely what kind of collaboration is here involved and the haunting suggestion, which
increases as one reads, of Fletcher in B and Beaumont and

Fletcher together in A. But this is beyond my commission. I did not set out to discover who perpetrated A, but only to declare my conviction – and give my reasons for the conviction – that Shakespeare was not guilty.

One word by way of postscript, in case it seems that I have dealt by implication too cavalierly with this seemingly Shakespearean style and its claim to be actually Shakespeare's writing. A further reason for believing that it is not, is the disturbing fact that very often an image that recalls his style stands quite alone in a passage that does not;[1] or, more puzzling still, that it is sometimes embedded in,[2] derived from,[3] or servant to[4] a description or a thought which seems quite unlike him. Just what system of collaboration could produce this result it is hard to see. Even if we could imagine Shakespeare – as we could not – keeping a commonplace book to jot down images or turns of phrase, by what means did he or another plant these out in the text? One partner to a collaboration can hardly be supposed to hand his commonplace book to the other with an open invitation to use what suits him: nor is it easy to see how that other avails himself of this generous offer. Even if it were possible to attach images like seed pearls to passages with which, at the moment of jotting down, they had no connection, how can a large number of images, turns of syntax, or cadences be written *in vacuo*, unattached to any theme or subject? An intricate problem in artistic experience proposes itself here.

And this is not the end of the problem. For the relation between isolated patches of brilliance and the style in general is, though compatible with the supposition of imitation, unlike the corresponding relationship to Shakespeare's work, particularly of the late period. And when the unlikeness is paralleled by an equivalent disharmony (or at least unlikeness to Shakespeare's method) in the relation of style to thought and to the character it purports to reveal; of character to action; of

[1] III. ii. 63–5.   [2] I. iii. 9–10.   [3] I. i. 56–7.   [4] I. i. 160–2.

motive to event; and, finally, of that action and those events to the alleged tragic experience, we cannot but conclude that we are justified in seeing in this disharmony between the elements of the style and the total effect of the play a characteristic feature of *Two Noble Kinsmen* which is without parallel in any of Shakespeare's mature work. Perhaps, then, when all is said, our play is least like Shakespeare's work in precisely this fact, that the style is not strictly dramatic. That it lives, that is to say, in its own right and is not subordinated to the primary needs of the play as a play.[1]

[1] This paper was read at the Shakespeare Survey Conference, 1949. An additional note, attached to the typewritten copy, reads as follows – Add to illustration and analysis:

It is characteristic of this play (or of certain scenes) that the writer has no taste. He simply cannot discriminate between beauty and an ugliness which is not (either in context, relation, or use) the ugliness that Lessing rightly defends in art. As in these lines:

> Our Lords lie blistering in the visitating sun
> And were good kings when living.

The second line has a lovely cadence: that 'dying fall' that moves us so often in the best work of Beaumont and Fletcher jointly. But it is inseparably linked, syntactically and musically, to the hideous picture of the decomposing corpses – already talked about too much for the pathetic sentiment at which the scene aims to sustain them. It is absurd to say of any subject that it cannot be the matter of art. But it is possible to say of some, and in some connections, that they are destructive to that particular kind or piece of art. It is this utter insensitiveness to jarring juxtaposition that marks the transitions from beauty of phrasing, image, syntax, or cadence to the ugly or repulsive in picture, image, or reference, that stamps the mark of the playwright of the doubtful scenes of *T.N.K.* Now these habits may or may not be Fletcher's (myself, I think they are), but that they are not Shakespeare's there is 'no manner of doubt whatever'.

(U.E.-F., although continuing to deny Shakespeare's part-authorship of the play, was not in 1957 as positive as she had been. It is arguable that the ugliness of the first of the above lines is necessary in order to convey the urgency of the Queen's request.)

Index

Index

Racine, 5, 84, 99, 123

Shakespeare: *Antony*, 6, 8, 12, 85, 87; *All's Well*, 129; *Coriolanus*, 48, 60, 132, 141, 148; *Cymbeline*, 131, 182; *Hamlet*, 39, 52, 98, 107, 111, 148, 153; *Henry IV*, 6, 47, 57, 103, 111, 113; *Henry V*, 6, 117; *Henry VIII*, 182; *Lear*, 39, 57; *Macbeth*, 4, 17, 30, 43, 58, 93, 118, 126; *Midsummer Night's Dream*, 81, 86; *Measure*, 45, 121, 129, 130; *Much Ado*, 6, 116, 119; *Othello*, 4, 101, 118; *Pericles*, 182; *Richard II*, 6, 18; *Richard III*, 117; *Tempest*, 111; *Timon*, 158, 178; *Troilus*, 103, 127, 162, 166; *Two Gentlemen*, 111; *Winter's Tale*, 131, 182

Sophocles, 4, 7, 8, 11, 84

Spurgeon, Caroline, 126

Terence, 119

Two Noble Kinsmen, 177 ff.

Webster, 1, 5, 111

Wilder, Thornton, 14

Yeats, 2